Cambridge Elements

Cambridge Elements in International Economics
edited by
Kenneth A. Reinert
George Mason University

BREAKING OR BUILDING BRIDGES?

The Trade Story of the MENA Region

Fida Karam
Gulf University for Science and Technology

Chahir Zaki
University of Orléans and Economic Research Forum

CAMBRIDGE
UNIVERSITY PRESS

Shaftesbury Road, Cambridge CB2 8EA, United Kingdom

One Liberty Plaza, 20th Floor, New York, NY 10006, USA

477 Williamstown Road, Port Melbourne, VIC 3207, Australia

314–321, 3rd Floor, Plot 3, Splendor Forum, Jasola District Centre,
New Delhi – 110025, India

103 Penang Road, #05–06/07, Visioncrest Commercial, Singapore 238467

Cambridge University Press is part of Cambridge University Press & Assessment,
a department of the University of Cambridge.

We share the University's mission to contribute to society through the pursuit of
education, learning and research at the highest international levels of excellence.

www.cambridge.org
Information on this title: www.cambridge.org/9781009516358

DOI: 10.1017/9781009516334

When citing this work, please include a reference to the DOI 10.1017/9781009516334

First published 2026

A catalogue record for this publication is available from the British Library

ISBN 978-1-009-51635-8 Hardback
ISBN 978-1-009-51636-5 Paperback
ISSN 2753-9326 (online)
ISSN 2753-9318 (print)

Breaking or Building Bridges?

The Trade Story of the MENA Region

Cambridge Elements in International Economics

DOI: 10.1017/9781009516334
First published online: April 2026

Fida Karam
Gulf University for Science and Technology

Chahir Zaki
University of Orléans and Economic Research Forum

Author for correspondence: Fida Karam, karam.f@gust.edu.kw

Abstract: This Element presents the main characteristics of international trade in the Middle East and North Africa (MENA) region by analyzing whether its trade policy managed to build or break bridges among MENA countries and with the rest of the world. Its objective is threefold. First, it provides an overview of trade theories from the MENA region perspective. Second, it analyzes the main trends and features of trade flows and trade policies. Third, it shows how trade policies had different development outcomes related to gender, informal employment, and the composition of labor demand. The main findings show that trade policies and domestic characteristics explain the relatively poor performance of trade flows in most of the diversified MENA economies. Also, the MENA region is highly affected by world business cycles, given that this region is the largest exporter of oil. Finally, development outcomes still need to be streamlined within trade policies.

Keywords: trade policy, MENA region, trade theories, international trade, institutions

ISBNs: 9781009516358 (HB), 9781009516365 (PB), 9781009516334 (OC)
ISSNs: 2753-9326 (online), 2753-9318 (print)

Contents

1 Introduction

The Middle East and North Africa (MENA) region,[1] gathering countries with different cultures, languages, and economic conditions, plays an important role in the global economy due to its strategic location, its abundant natural resources, and historical significance as a crossroads of trade. The region is located at the crossroads of Europe, Asia, and Africa, making it a vital commerce junction. It is abundant in natural resources, particularly oil and natural gas, therefore playing a significant role in the global energy market. Moreover, it is home to some of the world's earliest civilizations that developed sophisticated trade networks and maritime routes, contributing to the region's historical significance as a trade hub.

Indeed, the famous ancient Silk Road and Incense Route, which facilitated the exchange of goods and cultures between the East and the West, passed through the MENA region. The Silk Road connecting China with the Mediterranean passed through MENA cities such as Aleppo in Syria and was famous for trading silk, spices, precious stones, and other luxury goods. The Incense Route, connecting the Arabian Peninsula with the Mediterranean, was known for the trade of frankincense, myrrh, and other valuable goods from Yemen and Oman. During the Islamic Golden Age, between the eighth and fourteenth centuries, the MENA region in general, and Baghdad in particular, became a hub of intellectual, cultural, and economic activities. Later, the Ottoman Empire established trade networks connecting Europe to India and China and passing through MENA cities. MENA's ports, such as Alexandria and Basra, played significant roles in facilitating the maritime trade of spices, textiles, and precious metals.

Despite the region's pivotal role in trade and the global economy, MENA's economic growth is highly volatile due to oil price volatility and political instability. Indeed, MENA's oil exporters are heavily dependent on oil and hydrocarbon revenues, therefore witnessing rapid growth during periods of high oil prices, and economic slowdowns during periods of low oil prices. To

---

[1] The MENA region gathers the following twenty-one countries from the Middle East and North Africa: Algeria, Bahrain, Djibouti, Egypt, Iran, Iraq, Israel, Jordan, Kuwait, Lebanon, Libya, Malta, Morocco, Oman, West Bank and Gaza, Qatar, Saudi Arabia, Syria, Tunisia, United Arab Emirates, and Yemen. A map of the region is provided in Figure A.1 in the Appendix. Regarding the inclusion of Malta and Israel, we acknowledge that these two economies differ structurally from some other MENA countries, particularly in terms of trade openness, economic diversification, and income levels. However, we note that their inclusion reflects the reality that both countries are geographically located within the broader MENA sphere and actively participate in regional trade and economic dynamics. Malta, as a Mediterranean economy, maintains trade linkages with North Africa and the broader Middle East. Israel, likewise, has growing trade and investment ties with MENA countries, especially after recent normalization agreements.

this is added political instability and ongoing conflicts that disrupt trade and investment, hindering the growth prospects in the region.

Therefore, over the past few decades, the MENA region deployed serious efforts to implement economic reforms that promote sustainable growth, focusing on export-led strategies and trade liberalization. Oil-exporting countries, particularly in the Gulf Cooperation Council (GCC),[2] have engaged in diversification strategies to mitigate dependency on oil exports. Oil-importing countries in the region have focused on being more competitive in sectors like agriculture, tourism, and manufacturing. Trade liberalization measures, such as the reduction of tariff and nontariff barriers, and trade facilitation initiatives, have been implemented to promote trade openness. Moreover, MENA countries have joined different bilateral and regional trade agreements to enhance trade flows among neighboring countries. Examples include the Greater Arab Free Trade Area (GAFTA) aiming at promoting trade openness among Arab countries, and the Euro-Mediterranean Trade Agreement between the European Union and multiple Mediterranean countries.

To what extent are MENA's efforts effective in building bridges? In other words, to what extent are MENA countries deploying efforts to connect and integrate both regionally and globally? And could some countries be, unintentionally or deliberately, taking actions that break those bridges and hinder the desired regional global integration? While there have been notable achievements in fostering regional and global integration through trade liberalization measures and free trade agreements, significant challenges remain. Political instability, protectionist measures especially for service trade, and limited diversification continue to hinder the full potential of trade policies in the region. To answer clearly these questions, one should keep in mind that the MENA region encompasses countries with varying economic conditions, income levels, and trade performance. Indeed, oil-rich countries, in particular GCC countries possess abundant oil and gas reserves, enjoy higher per capita income levels due to oil revenues, and have more substantial financial reserves to invest in infrastructure projects, support the diversification of their economies away from fossil fuels and enhance their competitiveness on international markets. Non-oil countries, on the other hand, are more diversified but often have lower per capita income levels and face greater economic challenges, such as limited investment opportunities, relatively poor infrastructure, higher unemployment rates, and, in some countries, political instability. Trade policies can also differ significantly between oil exporters and importers due to their contrasting economic structures, trade dependencies, and development policies.

---

[2] GCC countries are Bahrain, Kuwait, Oman, Qatar, Saudi Arabia, and the United Arab Emirates.

Therefore, accounting for those differences between countries is crucial for understanding the trade dynamics in the MENA region.

This Element tells the story of trade in the MENA region, exploring historical backgrounds, the applicability of international trade theories, trade patterns and policies, as well as the relation between trade and economic growth. It is structured as follows: Section 2 explains why this region is rather heterogeneous. Section 3 looks at the history of trade policies in the MENA region, differentiating between resource-rich and poor countries as well as between labor-abundant and labor-importing countries. Section 4 provides a brief overview of international trade theories and their applicability to the MENA region. Section 5 delves into trade patterns at the macro level, distinguishing between trade in goods and services, and explores the concentration of MENA trading partners. Section 6 analyzes the influence of trade on the behavior and performance of firms. Section 7 provides some potential explanations of trade patterns, looking at trade policies and other factors affecting trade such as conflicts and institutional quality. Section 8 examines the link between trade, growth, and business cycles. Section 9 explores the role of trade in shaping development outcomes in the MENA region. Section 10 concludes, and Section 11 provides some policy implications.

Delving into the heterogeneous characteristics of MENA countries can indeed illuminate the applicability of various trade theories, helping to explain trade flows at both macro and micro levels. Moreover, since trade policies, conflicts, and institutional quality are critical factors shaping trade flows in the region, by understanding these factors, one can have a better picture of the complex trade environment in the region – that is highly affected by world business cycles – and recommend strategies to enhance trade relations and economic growth. Based on our analysis of trade in the MENA region, several key conclusions emerge: First, the MENA region experienced liberalization without real integration. Indeed, shallow trade agreements and persistent trade barriers, especially nontariff measures, high tariffs, and costly administrative barriers, in addition to weak institutions and lack of industrial competitiveness, explain the relatively poor performance of trade flows in most of the diversified MENA economies. Second, the MENA region is highly affected by the world business cycles given that the region is highly dependent on oil revenues. Therefore, in order to increase the region resilience, a stronger diversification should take place at the partners and the products levels. Moreover, trade policy should not be limited to the reduction of tariff barriers, but has to be broadened to other nontariff impediments, service regulations, and development-related issues, and should be accompanied by other reforms to improve the business environment and the quality of institutions and infrastructure.

2 A Heterogeneous Region

The MENA region consists of a heterogeneous group of countries that could be classified based on two notable country-related characteristics: the availability of oil resources and the size of their native populations. These country characteristics have shaped MENA's trade policies over the years. After offering a segmentation of the MENA region depending on countries' oil-exporting status and labor abundance, this section provides a comparison of MENA trade policies, focusing on the differences between oil-exporting vs. oil-importing countries, and labor-abundant vs. labor-importing countries after their independence.

The region encompasses countries with varying income levels, ranging from high-income to lower-income countries (World Bank Country Classification, 2024)[3]. This heterogeneity is even apparent between oil exporters, with GCC countries classified as high-income countries while other oil exporters are counted as upper-middle-income countries (Algeria, Iraq, and Libya), lower-middle income (Iran), and low income (Yemen). Oil importers are also heterogeneous in income levels. They combine high income countries (Israel and Malta), lower-middle income (Djibouti, Algeria, Egypt, Lebanon, Morocco and Tunisia), and low-income countries (Syria).

MENA oil-exporting countries are highly dependent on oil revenues. Indeed, oil exports account 65–95% of total exports in those countries, and oil revenues for more than 60% of their GDP (Karam and Zaki, 2015). GCC countries have the largest share of oil exports in total exports, with Kuwait (94.63%), Qatar (84.40%), and Saudi Arabia (77.49%) being on the top of the list in 2021 (WDI, 2024).

One structural factor that helps explain why some oil-rich countries remain middle- to lower-income despite abundant natural resources is the phenomenon of Dutch disease, which has profoundly shaped their economic and trade trajectories. The Dutch disease describes the structural economic distortions that arise when resource-rich countries experience large inflows of revenues from oil and gas exports, leading to real exchange rate appreciation and a decline in competitiveness in sectors such as manufacturing and agriculture. This phenomenon became particularly visible following the 1973 oil crisis and the subsequent rise in global oil prices, when resource-rich countries witnessed massive increases in oil revenues.

During this period, public investment and government consumption in these countries expanded rapidly, often financed by oil revenues. However, while GCC countries later used sovereign wealth funds and external investments to partially mitigate Dutch disease effects, much of this spending in non-GCC resource-rich

---

[3] https://datahelpdesk.worldbank.org/knowledgebase/articles/906519-world-bank-country-and-lending-groups.

countries was directed toward non-tradable sectors (such as construction, services, and government employment) rather than supporting the development of a diversified manufacturing base. For instance, Algeria pursued ambitious industrialization programs in the 1970s that ultimately failed to create a competitive export sector outside hydrocarbons, due in part to a loss of price competitiveness caused by an appreciated real exchange rate. Similarly, Iraq in the late 1970s used oil revenues for massive infrastructure and military build-up, but its non-oil sectors remained weak and heavily dependent on government demand. Iran also exhibited symptoms of Dutch disease where a booming oil sector fueled rapid urbanization and service sector expansion in the 1970s, but agricultural and manufacturing competitiveness eroded, contributing to rural discontent and structural vulnerabilities that became evident after the 1979 revolution. Libya under Gaddafi, especially during the 1970s and early 1980s, used oil revenues to fund vast public sector employment and social programs, yet developed little export capacity beyond oil, leaving it highly exposed to oil market fluctuations.

The symptoms of Dutch disease have persisted into the 2000s and 2010s. For example, despite periods of high oil prices (such as 2004–2014), Algeria's non-hydrocarbon exports continued to account for less than 5% of total exports. Iraq, after decades of conflict and sanctions, continues to rely on oil for more than 90% of government revenue and exports, with limited progress in building a competitive non-oil economy.

While lacking natural resources, many oil importers are abundant in human resources due to the size of their native populations. The most populated oil-importing countries in the region are Egypt, Morocco, and Syria (WDI, 2024). Some oil exporters are also labor abundant. Indeed, Iran, Algeria, Iraq, and Yemen appear among the most populated countries in the region. Abundance of human resources presents opportunities for economic growth and development, by increasing labor supply, which translates to lower labor costs, and can lead to higher output and productivity, particularly in labor-intensive sectors. Moreover, a larger population means a higher demand for goods and services, which can stimulate economic growth. Nevertheless, it is noteworthy that labor abundance poses challenges that require effective policy responses, such as investment in education, skill development, infrastructure, and job creation initiatives.

Therefore, we are inspired from Diop et al. (2012)[4] to classify MENA countries based on their oil export status and labor abundance according to

---

[4] Syria is classified by Diop et al. (2012) as a resource-rich, labor-abundant country. However, the International Monetary Fund (IMF) classifies Syria as an oil-importing country. We follow the IMF classification for two reasons: first, Syria's oil production and oil reserves are low compared with other resource-rich countries. Second, the sanctions imposed on the Syrian economy since 2011 have prohibited imports of oil produced or originated from Syria.

the following their categories: resource-poor labor-abundant countries, resource-rich labor-abundant countries and resource-rich labor-importing countries (Table 1). To ensure full coverage of all MENA countries in the analysis, we add a fourth category for resource-poor labor-importing countries. To summarize, MENA countries are classified as follows:

Table 1 MENA countries' characteristics, 2022

	Fuel exports (% of total merchandise exports)	Population	GDP/capita
Resource-Poor Labor-Abundant Countries:			
Egypt	35.95	110990103	4295.41
Jordan	0.92	11285869	4311.00
Lebanon	0.43	5489739	3823.94
Morocco	1.01	37457971	3441.99
Syria	N/A	22125249	N/A
Tunisia	8.03	12356117	3607.91
WBG	0.05	5043612	3799.96
Resource-Rich Labor-Abundant Countries:			
Algeria	N/A	44903225	5023.25
Iraq	N/A	44496122	6441.92
Iran	47.91*	88550570	4668.46
Libya	94.41**	6812341	8211.38
Yemen	0.14**	33696614	698.85
Resource-Rich Labor-Importing Countries:			
Bahrain	0.04	1472233	30146.93
Kuwait	96.04	4268873	42823.83
Oman	74.04	4576298	25056.79
Qatar	87.29	2695122	87480.42
Saudi Arabia	77.50*	36408820	30447.88
UAE	73.14	9441129	53707.98
Resource-Poor Labor-Importing Countries:			
Israel	5.32	9557500	54930.94
Malta	4.92	531113	34563.40

Source: World Bank, World Development Indicators database online, 2024.

Note: (i) GDP/capita is in current $US. (ii) UAE: United Arab Emirates; WBG: West Bank & Gaza.

*For Iran and Saudi Arabia, the value for the share of fuel exports is for 2021.

**For Libya and Yemen, the value for the share of fuel exports is for 2019.

- resource-poor labor-abundant countries: Egypt, Jordan, Lebanon, Morocco, Syria, Tunisia, and West Bank and Gaza.
- resource-rich labor-abundant countries: Algeria, Iran, Iraq, Libya,[5] and Yemen.
- resource-rich labor-importing countries: Bahrain, Kuwait, Oman, Qatar, Saudi Arabia, and United Arab Emirates (GCC countries).
- resource-poor labor-importing countries: Israel and Malta.

3 Historical Background

The trade policies of MENA countries have been defined based on their development needs. The region drew inspiration from other countries in shaping its industrialization strategies. Initially, many MENA countries adopted, after their independence, import substitution industrialization (ISI) policies, aimed at reducing dependency on foreign goods by fostering domestic industries. However, over time, these countries began to shift toward export-oriented policies, recognizing the benefits of integrating into the global economy and boosting their international trade.[6]

3.1 Import Substitution Strategies (1950s–1970s)

In the early years after their independence, most MENA countries adopted import substitution industrialization strategies (ISI) (Bruton, 1998), that gained popularity in the middle of the last century, aiming at reducing dependence on imported products by promoting domestic production. ISI policies emphasized the importance of state-owned enterprises, authorized favorable tax treatment for some private investments, high tariffs and quotas on imported goods to protect nascent domestic industries. These ISI strategies varied between oil importers and oil exporters depending on the structure of their economies and their domestic industries (Galal, 2008).

The trade policies of resource-rich labor-importing countries have been shaped by their reliance on oil exports and the use of oil revenues to import a wide range of products needed for their development. Therefore, their trade policies were shaped to facilitate the import of goods and services necessary for their development and diversification strategies: tariffs were low on consumer goods and raw materials but high on goods that could compete with local

---

[5] Beyond population size, Libya is considered labor-abundant because of the large surplus of labor relative to the limited capacity of its non-oil productive sectors, leading to widespread under-employment. In contrast, Saudi Arabia is classified as labor-importing due to its structural reliance on foreign workers, who make up the majority of the private sector workforce, reflecting a persistent gap between domestic labor supply and economic demand.

[6] Table A.1 in the appendix highlights the ISI period for each MENA country before adopting an export-oriented industrialization (EOI) strategy.

industries that the government aims to promote as part of the diversification strategy (Hvidt, 2013).

Recognizing the vulnerability of being heavily reliant on oil exports, oil exporters leveraged oil revenues to diversify their economies by developing non-oil industries. Given the limited labor force, these countries, especially GCC countries, set up state-owned enterprises and focused on developing strategic capital-intensive industries such as petrochemicals and refining industries, steel, cement and aluminum. Examples include the establishment of Saudi Basic Industries Corporation in 1976 in Saudi Arabia, aimed at producing petrochemicals domestically, and Kuwait National Petroleum Company and Kuwait Petroleum Corporation to develop the domestic refining capacity in Kuwait and expand petrochemical production. Qatar leveraged its vast natural gas reserves to develop a domestic petrochemical industry. Saudi Arabia invested in steel and cement production to meet domestic construction needs, reducing reliance on imports, while Kuwait invested in local production of construction materials like cement to support the booming construction sector. While the ISI helped in laying the foundation for industrial development, state-owned enterprises often suffered from inefficiencies and lacked competitiveness compared to global standards. In addition, reliance on oil revenues to fund industrial projects made those countries vulnerable to fluctuations in oil prices.

In addition to using oil revenues to develop capital intensive industries such as petrochemicals, steel, automotive, and consumer goods, resource-rich labor-abundant countries have made use of their large labor forces, to foster labor-intensive industries as well, such as textiles, construction materials, and food processing. Algeria and Iran, capitalizing on their large labor forces, have invested in spinning, weaving, and garment production to help build capacity for further growth in the textile and apparel sector. Given the need for reconstruction and infrastructure development (especially in Iraq and Libya), labor-intensive construction materials industries, such as cement, steel, and ceramics, are significant in Algeria, Iran, and Iraq. Algeria, Iran, and Yemen have developed their food processing industry, from agriculture to packaging and logistics, contributing to job creation and reducing dependence on food imports. Traditional handicrafts and small-scale manufacturing (such as leather goods, pottery, and carpets) remain vital for preserving cultural heritage in Yemen and Libya, while creating job opportunities mainly in rural areas.

Resource-poor labor-abundant economies are usually diversified but often suffer from trade deficits due to the fluctuation of the price of energy that they need to import. In those countries, ISI strategies led to the establishment of a variety of industries that are mainly labor intensive such as textiles and other consumer goods. The state established state-owned enterprises with substantial state support, in strategic sectors such as steel, textiles, cement, and chemicals, and imposed high tariff rates as well as nontariff barriers such as import quotas on the imports of those products. For instance, Egypt focused on developing its steel industry and the manufacturing of consumer goods and textiles. Jordan developed its phosphate mining and cement industries to utilize local resources and reduce imports. The country also developed its food processing industry to add value to agricultural products and reduce dependency on imported foodstuffs. Morocco invested in textiles and apparel industry, as well as in processed agricultural products, such as canned goods and beverages, reducing reliance on imported food items. Tunisia focused on developing consumer goods such as electronics, home appliances, and textiles. Lebanon focused on developing light manufacturing industries, such as textiles, garments, and food processing.

ISI strategies in resource-poor labor-importing countries played a crucial role in diversifying the economy and decreasing dependency on imported products. Israel focused on developing domestic industries, particularly in manufacturing and agriculture, to produce goods locally that were previously imported. ISI policies in Malta led to promoting sectors such as textiles, food processing, and manufacturing, reducing dependency on traditional sectors like agriculture and services (Briguglio, 1995).

While ISI strategies helped lay the foundation for industrial development, state-owned enterprises often suffered from inefficiencies and lacked competitiveness. Moreover, heavy dependence on state support and protectionist measures led to a lack of innovation within domestic industries and made them uncompetitive internationally. As a result, countries faced difficulties in expanding their export markets beyond primary commodities. In addition, ISI often led to persistent balance of payments problems for resource-poor countries: indeed, while the import of consumer goods decreased, the need for imports of machinery, raw materials, and intermediate goods increased, straining foreign exchange reserves. Therefore, ISI was costly to maintain, resulting in debt crises. At the same time, the export-oriented strategies adopted by East Asian economies gained popularity due to their proven success in driving economic growth and industrialization. Those strategies mainly focused on human capital development and strategic investments in education to meet the specific needs of the export-driven economy and enabled the East Asian Tigers to develop a skilled and competitive workforce that survived global competition and contributed to rapid economic growth. The East Asian experience inspired MENA countries, among other developing countries, to use export-oriented policies as the centerpiece of their development strategies.

3.2 Export-Oriented Strategies

With the failure of ISI similar to other developing countries, MENA countries have engaged in trade reforms in the 1990s, relying on export-oriented strategies to boost economic growth. Trade policy has shifted to lower tariff rates, more simplified export and import procedures, the elimination of export licensing requirements, and reduction or suppression of import quotas. Many countries, especially resource-poor ones, have signed in to structural adjustment programs, to secure a loan from the International Monetary Fund and/or the World Bank, where they agree to a set of economic reforms, including reducing government spending, and trade liberalization. For instance, Morocco, Tunisia, and Jordan were among the first countries to implement a structural adjustment program (in 1983, 1986 and 1989 respectively), taking measures to liberalize their trade. Egypt followed in 1990–1991. Kuwait has adopted trade liberalization measures in the aftermath of its membership to the World Trade Organization (WTO) in 1995, as well as Oman in 1996 and Saudi Arabia after the mid-1980s (Droguel and Tekce, 2011). Up to the present time, 13 MENA countries are WTO members.[7]

In the context of export-oriented strategies, it is important to acknowledge that many MENA countries have historically pursued a price-competitiveness approach, primarily by maintaining low labor costs and undervalued exchange rates to stimulate export growth. However, as highlighted by Rodrik (2005), such strategies have often failed to generate sustained export diversification or productivity gains in the absence of strong institutional foundations. Structural problems such as weak governance and inadequate support for innovation, have constrained the effectiveness of price-based strategies. This has left many countries locked into low-value-added export sectors, unable to transition toward more sophisticated, knowledge-intensive industries.

To achieve meaningful export growth, MENA countries had to secure international markets to their products, to benefit from economies of scale that are difficult to achieve on narrow domestic markets. Therefore, countries signed in a variety of bilateral and multilateral trade agreements with each other, African states, the European Union (EU), the United States (US), and Turkey (Rouis and Tabor, 2013).

Examples of regional trade agreements include the GAFTA, the Agadir Agreement, and the GCC. GAFTA is a regional trade agreement established in 1997 under the auspices of the Arab League, aimed at promoting economic integration among its members by reducing trade barriers. It was founded

---

[7] Bahrain, Djibouti, Egypt, Israel, Jordan, Kuwait, Malta, Morocco, Oman, Qatar, Saudi Arabia, Tunisia, and the United Arab Emirates.

initially by seventeen countries: Jordan, Iraq, Saudi Arabia, Kuwait, Yemen, Lebanon, Egypt, Bahrain, Libya, Oman, Qatar, Syria, Morocco, Sudan, Tunisia, the UAE, and Palestine, with Algeria joining in 2005. The agreement, which entered into force in 2005, seeks to foster economic cooperation among member states and increase intra-regional trade through the elimination tariffs, customs duties, and other trade restrictions on goods. Therefore, GAFTA aims to boost economic growth, diversify Arab economies, and reduce their dependence on non-Arab trading partners. However, many challenges persist, including political differences and varying levels of economic development among member states (for instance, Sudan and Yemen are less developed than the other members), and the existence of nontariff barriers. Despite these challenges, GAFTA remains a strategic step toward achieving greater economic integration and cooperation within the Arab world (Abedini and Peridy, 2008).

The Agadir Agreement, signed in 2004 by Egypt, Jordan, Morocco, and Tunisia and entering into force in 2007, aims at fostering economic integration and trade cooperation among member countries. It seeks to create a free trade area by eliminating tariffs on industrial products, liberalizing agricultural trade and trade in services, and harmonizing customs procedures and standards. As a regional trade bloc, it also aims to strengthen economic ties between these countries and serves as a steppingstone toward greater economic integration with the EU through the Euro-Mediterranean partnership, which offers access to European Union markets (Droguel and Tekce, 2011). While the agreement has achieved some success in boosting trade among member countries, challenges persist, such as bureaucratic procedures at the border, nontariff barriers, and different levels of economic development between members.

The GCC is a regional political and economic alliance established in 1981 by six Gulf Arab states: Bahrain, Kuwait, Oman, Qatar, Saudi Arabia, and the United Arab Emirates, aiming at fostering economic, political, security, and cultural cooperation among its members. The GCC has pursued initiatives such as a customs union, a common market, and plans for a monetary union to enhance economic integration. In 2003, GCC became a customs union and a common market in 2008, implementing free trade among the members, with common tariffs on imported goods from external trading partners, harmonizing development plans and adopting a common oil policy and coordinating industrial policies. In addition to economic collaboration, the GCC also focuses on regional security, coordinating efforts at responding to regional conflicts and external threats.

In addition to trade agreements among the region's members, MENA countries have signed trade agreements with developed countries, mainly with the EU and the United States. Euro-Mediterranean Free Trade Agreements (EU-MED FTA) aim at enhancing political, economic and cultural cooperation between the EU and multiple Mediterranean countries in the MENA region. In this context, the agreement was signed by the EU with Tunisia in 1998, Morocco in 2000, Jordan in 2002, Egypt in 2004, Algeria in 2005, and Lebanon in 2006. As the Barcelona Process included the EU associated countries, the mentioned MENA countries have also negotiated/signed free trade agreements with Turkey. EU-MED FTA mainly focuses on the elimination of trade barriers, the adoption of common rules for the rules of origin, with limited liberalization in the agricultural sector (Droguel and Tekce, 2011).

Some countries have also signed a free trade agreement (FTA) with the US. The Jordan-US FTA is the first free trade agreement between the United States and an Arab country. It entered into force in 2001 and was fully implemented by 2010. The agreement seeks to gradually liberalize bilateral trade in goods and services between both parties. It covers a wide range of sectors, including agriculture, textiles, and services, and incorporates provisions regarding trade-related issues of the environment, labor, intellectual property rights, and the rules of origin, making it one of the first US trade agreements to include such standards. The agreement also aims to encourage US investment in Jordan, and support Jordan's broader economic reform and development goals. Since its implementation, the FTA has helped increase bilateral trade and investment, with significant growth in Jordan's exports to the US, particularly in the textiles and apparel sectors. The US-Jordan FTA is viewed as a model for trade agreements with other countries in the Middle East, such as the Morocco-US and Oman-US FTAs that entered into force in 2006 and 2009 respectively (Droguel and Tekce, 2011).

MENA's efforts in export-oriented industrialization have gone beyond trade agreements. Indeed, countries have been engaged in internal reforms and measures to boost exports in some key sectors. GCC countries, endowed with small populations but rich natural resources, have used oil revenues to invest in sectors such as petrochemicals, aluminum, steel, and plastics, and more recently in renewable energy, tourism, and financial services. Their trade policies have shifted to support this export orientation strategy by establishing free trade zones, and in some countries such as the UAE, allow full foreign ownership and minimal regulations to attract foreign investment. The UAE, especially Dubai, and, more recently, Saudi Arabia have become a major tourism destination. The UAE and Qatar have developed robust financial services sectors and established themselves as financial hubs. Qatar has focused on developing its natural gas industry, making it the world's largest exporter of liquefied natural gas.

Resource-rich, labor-abundant countries have also employed various export-oriented strategies to diversify their economies, reduce dependency on raw material exports, and harness their human capital for sustainable development. They focused on industries that add value to natural resources, such as petrochemicals, refining, and metals, and invested in various sectors away from oil, some that are labor-intensive like agriculture and textiles and other that are capital-intensive like automotive and electronics industries. Moreover, they have developed many services sectors, such as tourism, education services, banking and insurance services (in Algeria and Iran), medical tourism (in Iran), telecommunication services (in Libya and Yemen), and real estate (in Iraq and Libya). Most importantly, they have gone through regulatory reforms, created tax incentives, and established special economic zones to attract international companies. They have also invested in infrastructure to facilitate exports. Unfortunately, while much effort has been deployed by this group of countries, their export-oriented strategies have been significantly impacted by ongoing conflicts and political instability (Iraq, Yemen, and Libya), or by international sanctions (Iran).

Resource-poor, labor-abundant countries, endowed with relatively large, young, and often well-educated populations, have focused on leveraging their human capital by investing in education and vocational training to support export-oriented strategies. They often rely on labor migration to oil-abundant countries, with remittances playing a significant role in their economies. In this regard, their trade agreements often include provisions facilitating labor movement. Those countries focused on modernizing agriculture, and taking advantage of favorable climate and labor abundance, on promoting agricultural exports such as fruits, vegetables, and flowers. Moreover, they invested in light manufacturing industries, such as textiles, apparel, electronics, and automotive parts, to produce exportable products. They have also developed services sectors like tourism, information and communication technology (ICT) and software services, education, and healthcare. Like other countries, they established special economic zones by offering tax incentives, simplified regulations, and robust infrastructure, to attract foreign direct investment. For instance, Egypt, in addition to developing its textile and apparel industry, ICT sector, and tourism, has leveraged its agricultural potential to become a major exporter of fruits and vegetables. Jordan has developed a strong ICT sector, becoming a regional hub for technology and outsourcing services, and focused on tourism and key export sectors such as pharmaceutical products and garments. Tunisia has diversified its economy through the development of its automotive parts industry, electronics, textiles, and tourism. Morocco has focused on automotive manufacturing, electronics, and aerospace as key export industries. The country has also developed its agricultural exports, particularly in high-value crops such as citrus fruits and vegetables.

Resource-poor labor-importing countries, namely Israel and Malta, pursued export-oriented strategies to enhance the resilience of the economy. Israel has developed a strong high-tech sector and fostered a thriving ecosystem for startups, innovation, and entrepreneurship. The country has also promoted exports in other sectors such as agriculture, pharmaceuticals, and defense technology. With a competitive regulatory framework, tax incentives, a skilled workforce, and a strategic location in the Mediterranean, Malta has developed a strong services-oriented economy, promoting tourism and financial services.

Recognizing the limitations of ISI, and amid fluctuating global oil prices and other external shocks, MENA countries found in export-oriented strategies and diversification a remedy for their development challenges and an opportunity to build more resilient and sustainable economies through the integration of global markets and the attraction of foreign investment. How successful was this integration experience? Before delving into a detailed overview of MENA's trade flows and specialization, we offer in Section 4 a review of international trade theories and discuss their application to the MENA context.

4 A Refresher of International Trade Theories: MENA Perspective

International trade theories have evolved significantly over time, from classical concepts to contemporary models with more realistic assumptions capturing the complexity of trade patterns, therefore enhancing our understanding of international trade, and guiding policy decisions that can foster economic growth and development. Accordingly, a brief review of the evolution of international trade theories is necessary to elucidate the dynamics of trade patterns and trade policies in the MENA region.

Classical and neoclassical trade theories evaluate the competitiveness of a country by its exogenous factor endowments. Classical theories and represented by the Theory of Absolute Advantage of Adam Smith in 1776 and Ricardo's Comparative Advantage theory in 1817. The Theory of Absolute Advantage argues that free trade would lead to increased overall wealth and efficiency if countries specialize in producing goods where they have an absolute advantage that they can produce more efficiently than other countries (Smith, 1776), The applicability of the absolute advantage theory was questioned in the case of a dominant country with an absolute advantage in all goods that would not benefit from international trade. Consequently, Ricardo's Theory of Comparative Advantage expanded Smith's model and argued that trade between a dominant country and a country with no absolute advantage can still benefit both countries, if each country specializes in goods where they have the lowest opportunity cost (Ricardo, 1817). In Ricardo's model, labor is the sole production factor, and countries have different technologies that explain the difference in their productivity levels. However, Ricardo did not explain why technology levels should be considered as exogenous.

Graham (1923) argued that the Theory of Comparative Advantage may lead to suboptimal specialization when one sector exhibits increasing returns to scale (such as manufacturing) and another exhibits diminishing returns (such as agriculture or resource extraction), even when potential gains exist in manufacturing sectors that exhibit increasing returns to scale. If a country specializes according to its existing comparative advantage in the diminishing returns sector, it may forego long-term gains from developing the increasing returns sector. Thus, under free trade, economies might be locked into inferior development paths, justifying temporary protection for emerging industries. This argument laid an early foundation for the infant-industry protection rationale and has been a cornerstone of development economics, particularly for countries seeking to industrialize after being locked into primary commodity exports.

Neoclassical trade theories were built on the principles of classical theories, emphasizing the role of comparative advantage, resource allocation, and market equilibrium. The Heckscher-Ohlin model (1933) highlights the role of a country's factor endowments in determining its production cost and therefore its comparative advantage. Technology is similar between countries, but production methods differ due to different combinations of production factors. According to this model, a country will export the goods that use its abundant factors intensively and import the goods that use its scarce factors intensively. The Stolper-Samuelson Theorem (Stolper and Samuelson, 1941) uses the Heckscher-Ohlin model to examine the impact of trade on income distribution within countries and provides insight into the political economy of trade policy. It shows that free trade benefits the factor of production that a country has in abundance and harms the scarce factor.

How do classical and neoclassical trade theories manifest in the context of the MENA region? Almost half of MENA countries, and especially GCC countries, are abundant in fossil fuels. Benefiting from this comparative advantage, those countries export oil and oil derivatives to other countries lacking these natural resources. Data from the US Energy Information Administration[8] shows that the MENA region includes five of the top ten oil-producing countries (Saudi

---

Arabia, Iraq, United Arab Emirates, Iran, Kuwait) and is responsible for producing about 26% of world production. Except for Iran that suffers from international sanctions, the previous countries are also featured among the major oil-exporting countries. By contrast, MENA non-oil exporters like Egypt, Morocco, and Tunisia are known for their significant labor resources due to various factors such as population size, education levels, and workforce participation rates. That being so, they have a comparative advantage in traditional sectors like agriculture and textiles, as well as tourism due to their geographic conditions, and low labor cost. Moreover, Graham's argument resonates strongly in many MENA countries, where resource abundance has led to strong dependency on oil and gas exports and limited industrial diversification. For instance, Algeria, Iraq, and Libya have specialized in oil and gas sectors that exhibit diminishing returns to scale and limited spillover effects. Despite possessing large labor forces and potential comparative advantages in labor-intensive manufacturing, these countries became heavily reliant on hydrocarbon exports, which discouraged the development of industries with increasing returns, such as textiles, light manufacturing, or agro-processing. Similarly, the infant-industry argument is highly pertinent for many MENA economies, especially resource-rich, labor-abundant countries such as Algeria, Iraq, or Iran, who have struggled to develop competitive manufacturing sectors due to early exposure to international competition and a lack of sustained policy support. Without temporary protection and sound industrial policies, industries with potential economies of scale have to compete internationally.

The Specific Factor Model, developed by Jones (1971) and Samuelson (1971), builds on classical trade theory by introducing the idea that while some factors of production (like labor) are mobile across sectors, others (like capital) are "specific" to particular industries and cannot move easily. In this framework, an economy is composed of multiple sectors, each relying on a specific, immobile factor and a common mobile factor. Changes in trade patterns, prices, or external shocks affect the income distribution between sectors, because specific factors benefit or suffer depending on how their sector is impacted. Applying this to resource-rich MENA countries, when the price of oil rises, the oil sector becomes more profitable. Labor, being mobile, moves toward the booming sector to benefit from higher wages, and workers who stay in the sectors not experiencing the boom (like manufacturing or agriculture) may face declining wages, and the specific factors in those sectors (like agricultural land or industrial machinery) earn lower returns compared to before the shock. Therefore, the Specific Factor Model helps explain the Dutch disease that has profoundly shaped most resource-rich MENA economies, distorting their economic development toward hydrocarbons sectors, and away from other sectors, that are often critical for long-term economic growth and diversification.

Critics argue that neoclassical trade theories rely on simplified assumptions that are not very realistic, such as the assumptions of perfectly competitive markets, factor mobility internally but not internationally, constant returns to scale and the absence of transport costs. Moreover, the static nature of comparative advantage does not account for dynamic gains from trade, such as technological advancement and innovation. The postwar period to the late 1970s was characterized by a rapid growth and structural changes in international trade among industrial countries, leading to modern trade theories recognizing the importance of economies of scale and imperfect competition in the analysis of trade.

Expanding on neoclassical theories, Krugman (1979) introduced a pivotal framework that highlights how technological leadership in certain industries (usually in developed countries) creates a "leader-follower" dynamic, which can be important for understanding the trade patterns and development outcomes of countries. In Krugman's model, countries that are more technologically advanced (the leaders) enjoy greater productivity and competitive advantages in certain industries, which allow them to dominate those markets. On the other hand, follower countries may lack the same technological capacity, leading to lower productivity and a reliance on resource extraction or simple manufacturing rather than high-tech industries. This gap can widen over time, especially in economies that don't invest in technological innovation or education.

Krugman's model can be applied to many MENA countries, particularly those that are resource-rich. These countries often face a significant gap in technological innovation compared to more advanced economies, which limits their ability to diversify and develop competitive manufacturing or high-tech sectors. As a result, they remain heavily dependent on natural resource exports, such as oil and gas, rather than fostering industries that could drive long-term growth. They may experience difficulty in bridging this technological gap, leading to a reliance on low-value-added sectors and hindering economic diversification.

The New Trade Theory was developed by Paul Krugman in 1980, arguing that trade between countries is driven not just by differences in resources or technology, but also by economies of scale and consumer preferences for variety, and highlighting the role of intra-industry trade (trade in similar products) among similar countries. Krugman (1980) developed a general equilibrium model of Chamberlinian monopolistic competition where firms can achieve lower production costs through economies of scale and can also differentiate their products to capture different market segments. Intra-industry trade, therefore, occurs due to differentiated products and consumer preferences for variety. Krugman argues that industries with high fixed costs (such as like automobiles, electronics, or pharmaceuticals) benefit from producing on a larger scale. As production expands, average costs decrease, allowing firms to become more competitive globally.

When it comes to MENA countries, it is noteworthy that all countries have devoted substantial effort in designing their export-oriented strategies to benefit from economies of scale stemming from their access to international markets. Although to different extent, MENA countries invested heavily in technology and infrastructure, to improve their productivity and export competitiveness. The most famous examples are the main oil exporters, such as the UAE, Saudi Arabia, and Qatar, that have undertaken serious economic diversification strategies, to reduce dependence on oil and develop sectors where increasing returns to scale can be realized. Heavy investments have been made in renewable energy, financial services, technology, and tourism. Dubai International Financial Centre (DIFC) is an example of a financial hub consolidating financial activities in one location and facilitating economies of scale by accessing larger markets beyond the MENA region. The UAE and Saudi Arabia are investing in large-scale infrastructure projects, such as ports, logistics hubs, and free trade zones, that attract multinational businesses that leverage economies of scale and enhance competition in international markets.

Recent advancements in trade theory have focused on firm-level differences, instead of country differences, to explain variations in export performance across firms and industries. The "New-New Trade Theory" emerged with the seminal work of Melitz (2003) to highlight the importance of firm heterogeneity in terms of productivity and the existence of a fixed cost to enter export markets, in determining the number and the type of firms that become exporters as well as the gains from trade. Exporters have a productivity advantage before they start exporting – not as a result of exporting – because only the most productive firms are able to overcome the costs of entering export markets. Extensions of the Melitz's (2003) model explicitly account for the decision to export, that is, the extensive margin of trade (Chaney, 2008; Helpman et al., 2008; Melitz and Ottaviano, 2008).

The Melitz model provides a framework for understanding how firm heterogeneity influences trade dynamics in the MENA region. Indeed, most MENA countries have undertaken serious economic and trade reforms by reducing tariffs and nontariff barriers and made strenuous effort in trade integration by joining different bilateral and regional trade agreements. Increased competition due to access to other markets resulted in the exit of less productive firms while allowing more productive firms to access larger markets, where they can leverage their competitive advantages. For example, in countries like Morocco, Tunisia, and Egypt, the growth of export-oriented sectors like automotive parts, electronics, and agricultural products can be seen as an outcome of this dynamic. Energy companies in Qatar and the UAE have made substantial investments in technology and infrastructure necessary to survive global competitiveness. Additionally, both Qatar and the UAE have been trying to diversify their economies beyond oil and gas, with national strategies aimed at enhancing competitiveness and innovation. They have seen a growth in the number of firms exporting goods and services (like tourism, financial services, logistics, and high-tech industries). These firms have access to advanced technology, skilled labor, and efficient production processes, giving them a competitive edge in global markets.

Building on these theoretical foundations, we now turn to the gravity model, which, while rooted in economic theory, is primarily an empirical tool widely used to analyze actual trade flows and quantify the impact of various factors on international trade. The gravity model, initially developed by Tinbergen (1962) and Anderson (1979), has gained prominence in modern trade theory in analyzing bilateral trade between countries. It suggests that the volume of trade between two countries is directly proportional to their economic sizes and inversely proportional to the distance between them. The gravity model has undergone over years significant theoretical and empirical improvements (Mac Callum, 1995; Feenstra et al., 2001; Feenstra, 2002; Anderson and van Wincoop, 2003), enforcing its theoretical base, thus narrowing the gap between theoretical and empirical findings. It encompasses many determinants to predict trade patterns, such as GDP of both countries, their populations, geographical distance, whether they have a common border, whether they have a common language or a common colonial background, and whether they are both members of some trade agreements.

The gravity model provides a useful framework for understanding trade patterns in the MENA region. First, countries with larger economies, such as Saudi Arabia, the UAE, and Egypt, have significant trade volumes both within the region and with the rest of the world. Second, geographical proximity is a significant factor influencing trade patterns among MENA countries. Third, MENA countries share cultural and historical ties that enhance trade among them. Examples include the Arab Maghreb Union (AMU)[9] and countries of the Gulf Cooperation Council (GCC). Finally, and as discussed in the previous

---

[9] The Arab Maghreb Union (AMU) is a political union and economic trade agreement among Arab countries that are located primarily in the Maghreb. Its members are the nations of Algeria, Libya, Mauritania, Morocco, and Tunisia.

section, MENA countries have deployed much effort to promote regional trade integration, such as the GAFTA and the Agadir Agreement, to enhance trade among member countries. Some empirical studies have highlighted the role of other determinants of trade in the MENA region, such as the detrimental effect of war and conflicts (Karam and Zaki, 2016) and the role of institutional quality (Karam and Zaki, 2019). Moreover, Karam and Zaki (2013) used an augmented gravity model to investigate the trade performance in services of MENA countries. The authors are interested in each country's trade performance in services instead of bilateral service trade flows, and therefore adapt the gravity model to take into account unilateral variants of the variables that have been found in the literature to influence bilateral trade. They introduce a new determinant of trade performance, namely the number of bound commitments undertaken by a sector in the WTO as well as the availability of those commitments by mode of supply. After controlling for the possible selection bias coming from the fact that WTO bound commitments are only observed for WTO members, the authors found that, beyond traditional trade determinants, WTO membership and the number of bound commitments undertaken by a sector increase exports, imports and trade in services.

Different trade theories offer insights into the trade dynamics of MENA countries. The theory of comparative advantage explains their reliance on oil and gas export, while the New Trade Theory highlights their engagement in intra-industry trade in sectors such as manufacturing, driven by economies of scale and consumer demand for variety. The New-New Trade Theory highlights how trade liberalization efforts enable more productive firms to expand and less productive ones to exit, fostering overall economic efficiency. Together, these theories illustrate the region's evolving trade patterns shaped by resource endowments, economic reforms, and liberalization efforts. The following section delves into an overview of MENA trade flows to gain deeper insights into trade patterns at the region, country and sector levels, as well as MENA's key trading partners.

5 Overview of Trade Flows in the MENA Region: A Macro Approach

The trade performance of the MENA region appears to be mixed over time. Data from the World Development Indicators, 2023 show that the share of trade in MENA GDP increased substantially between 2000 (69%) and 2008 (91%), then stumbled in 2009 due to the financial crisis. Between 2009 and 2014, trade accounted for around 81–85% of MENA GDP. The share of trade in MENA GDP further decreased to 78% in 2015 due to collapsing oil prices, and to 69%

in 2020 and 60% in 2021 due to the COVID-19 pandemic. In 2022, as the world economy was starting to recover from the devastating effects of the pandemic, the share of trade in MENA GDP increased to 66%.

Figure 1 shows that in 2021[10] the share of trade in MENA GDP (60.12%) was almost comparable to high-income countries, and stood above the world average (56.79%) and above the share of trade in the GDP of middle-income countries. Indeed, the MENA region stands directly after Europe & Central Asia (with a share of 84.63%) and before the other regions, developed ones like North America (28.6%) as well as developing ones like sub-Saharan Africa (56.31%).

Exports account for 34.85% of MENA GDP and compare favorably, like the share of trade in the region's GDP, to all regions (except Europe & Central Asia), and especially to high and middle-income countries and the world's average. However, it is worth mentioning that this bright figure for MENA

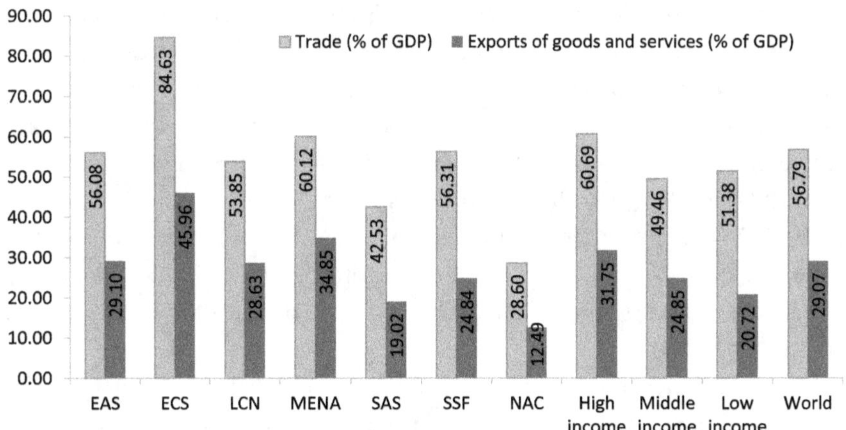

Figure 1 Trade as a percentage of GDP, 2021

Source: World Bank, World Development Indicators database online, 2024.

Note: (i) Trade is the sum of exports and imports divided by the value of GDP.
(ii) EAS: East Asia & Pacific; ECS: Europe & Central Asia; LCN: Latin America & Caribbean; MENA: Middle East & North Africa; SAS: South Asia; SSF: Sub-Saharan Africa; NAC: North America.

---

[10] We acknowledge the limitations of using 2021 data, as it reflects a period of partial recovery from the COVID-19 crisis. In some cases, trade and economic indicators may be temporarily elevated due to the rebound effect. However, 2021 remains the most recent year with complete and comparable data across all countries in the sample.

exports is mainly due to the region's heavy reliance on petroleum exports. Indeed, Karam and Zaki (2015) highlight that MENA trade excluding oil is at about the world average, but exports alone are below the world average. In addition, Behar and Freund (2011) show that, conditioning on GDP, distance, and a number of other factors, a typical MENA country under-trades with other countries: exports to the outside world are at only a third of their potential. However, intra-MENA trade is conditionally higher than extra-MENA trade. These results hold for aggregate exports, non-natural exports, and non-petroleum exports.

The region's average masks some heterogeneity at the country level. Table 2 shows that some countries like Saudi Arabia, Algeria, Iran, Iraq, Egypt, Israel, Lebanon, and Syria were behind the region's average share of trade in GDP in 2021 while other countries exceeded by far the region's average, such as Malta (315.31%), Djibouti (264.02%), the United Arab Emirates (UAE) (166.57% in 2020), and Bahrain (159.87%).

Another characteristic feature of trade's shares in GDP at the country level is their evolution over the years. While trade's share in GDP in many countries followed the region's pattern, some countries witnessed a decrease in trade's share in GDP while others saw an improvement in this share. For instance, in Libya, the share of trade in GDP doubled between 2000 (45%) and 2010 (98%) before dropping to 78% in 2019. In the UAE, trade's share in GDP moved up from 120% in 2005 to 167% in 2020. Iraq's share dropped expectedly following the war, from 125% in 2000 to 62% in 2021, and Yemen's share from 75% in 2000 to 59% in 2018 due to the devastating effects of the civil war. Similarly, Jordan saw its trade share in GDP declining from 110% in 2000 to 86% in 2019 (Table 2).

Expectedly, most oil exporters exceed the region's export share in GDP due to the high concentration of exports in petroleum products. The UAE and Bahrain show an export share in GDP that is double the region's average (95.93% in 2020 for the UAE and 89.68% for Bahrain in 2021 respectively). Despite being oil exporters, Algeria, Iran and Yemen exhibit export shares below the region's average: indeed, while Iran's oil exports are vulnerable to sanctions imposed by Western government, Yemen's civil war have had devastating effects on the economy and international trade since 2014. It is also noteworthy that oil-importing countries like Malta, Djibouti, and Tunisia exhibit higher shares of exports in GDP than the region's average. The share of exports in GDP in Malta (166.44%) and in Djibouti (143.02%) was more than four times the region's average in 2021.

Table 2 Total trade and exports as a percentage of GDP, by country (2000–2022)

MENA oil exporters		2000	2005	2010	2015	2016	2017	2018	2019	2020	2021	2022
GCC countries												
Bahrain	Total	135.81	148.31	120.47	154.93	139.62	143.09	150.81	141.70	140.22	159.87	..
	Exports	79.18	83.89	69.54	83.11	74.20	75.78	79.25	76.49	72.93	89.68	..
Kuwait	Total	86.62	92.24	97.03	98.70	96.16	97.84	103.12	98.18	..	..	..
	Exports	56.47	63.98	66.67	53.77	47.63	51.20	57.50	53.29	..	..	..
Oman	Total	92.90	99.11	96.39	96.38	82.86	88.95	89.28	86.48	91.88	93.92	..
	Exports	60.34	63.16	59.09	49.65	41.32	45.72	50.62	49.49	47.06	52.53	..
Qatar	Total	89.61	94.75	86.07	93.71	89.55	91.49	91.84	90.05	90.02	92.78	99.98
	Exports	67.28	65.09	62.32	57.06	47.71	52.89	55.94	52.19	49.12	58.73	68.44
Saudi Arabia	Total	68.17	81.95	82.55	69.50	59.91	61.81	61.96	60.20	49.71	57.14	63.51
	Exports	43.41	57.05	49.57	32.56	30.16	33.57	37.20	34.09	24.90	32.77	40.22
UAE	Total	..	119.55	138.89	169.48	170.90	172.80	157.92	167.38	166.57	..	..
	Exports	..	67.59	79.39	97.56	97.66	98.34	91.99	96.66	95.93	..	..

Table 2 (cont.)

MENA oil exporters		2000	2005	2010	2015	2016	2017	2018	2019	2020	2021	2022
Non-GCC countries												
Algeria	Total	62.86	71.28	69.87	59.70	55.93	55.32	58.07	51.81	45.33	53.20	59.04
	Exports	42.07	47.21	38.44	23.17	20.87	22.63	25.86	22.71	17.47	26.73	35.34
Iran	Total	41.26	54.44	43.77	39.42	40.39	44.74	58.57	50.75	43.81	44.37	51.60
	Exports	21.47	30.33	24.40	18.72	21.16	22.74	31.12	23.48	19.42	22.84	26.82
Iraq	Total	125.34	115.74	73.50	69.59	54.59	59.78	65.80	68.99	57.74	62.10	..
	Exports	75.70	54.35	39.42	34.51	28.11	33.92	40.80	38.05	27.75	37.68	..
Libya	Total	45.28	90.86	98.08	56.90	41.11	47.55	63.78	78.21	..	..	..
	Exports	31.56	63.72	66.27	22.23	14.58	27.20	39.61	42.84	..	..	..
Yemen	Total	75.44	76.77	64.39	31.64	32.65	44.95	58.90	..	..	..	..
	Exports	41.41	40.90	30.00	9.05	4.81	9.69	8.76	..	..	..	..
MENA oil importers												
Djibouti	Total	..	..	..	268.36	213.07	305.97	300.40	320.94	222.84	264.02	340.19
	Exports	..	..	..	145.42	103.76	150.10	156.62	166.72	115.63	143.02	169.00
Egypt	Total	39.02	62.95	47.94	34.85	30.25	42.83	45.91	41.12	32.13	29.86	36.98
	Exports	16.20	30.34	21.35	13.18	10.35	15.01	17.98	16.64	12.47	10.56	15.09
Israel	Total	69.30	79.13	66.44	59.21	58.04	56.56	58.89	56.27	50.96	55.19	60.50
	Exports	34.60	39.51	34.16	31.17	29.95	29.24	29.87	29.05	27.51	29.40	31.73
Jordan	Total	110.33	146.91	114.22	95.36	88.72	90.07	87.96	85.82	..	..	..
	Exports	41.83	52.70	47.00	36.54	34.40	34.71	35.13	36.67	..	..	..

Lebanon	Total	50.12	92.76	95.10	71.84	67.72	68.46	68.26	62.98	50.13	78.83	..
	Exports	14.18	36.62	35.02	23.14	21.73	21.93	20.75	20.70	16.37	26.03	..
Malta	Total	248.63	217.60	301.84	299.47	303.01	296.87	302.70	309.62	333.12	315.31	317.75
	Exports	120.25	103.58	150.95	154.62	157.80	158.10	160.70	163.94	173.77	166.44	165.29
Morocco	Total	53.44	61.49	69.54	67.29	71.12	74.17	77.25	76.00	68.84	75.63	101.12
	Exports	24.20	28.00	29.79	30.00	30.73	32.61	33.83	34.09	30.79	33.18	44.81
Syria	Total	65.28	80.13	64.01	51.09	67.11	61.05	50.66	42.00	48.40	97.85	..
	Exports	36.12	41.04	32.17	14.29	21.68	19.34	14.92	13.01	14.78	24.80	..
Tunisia	Total	82.64	90.25	100.15	87.25	87.09	95.81	103.87	100.94	82.82	92.94	110.74
	Exports	39.73	44.93	47.96	38.40	38.30	41.72	45.49	45.45	37.33	41.86	49.36
WBG	Total	87.64	83.84	68.50	70.78	65.42	68.45	71.40	68.99	67.29	73.08	85.90
	Exports	20.52	14.11	14.12	16.06	14.33	15.72	15.96	15.52	15.36	17.34	18.54

Source: World Bank, World Development Indicators database online, 2024.

Note: (i) Trade is the sum of exports and imports divided by the value of GDP.

(ii) UAE: United Arab Emirates; WBG: West Bank & Gaza.

5.1 Trade in Goods

Goods trade accounts for 48.6% of MENA GDP in 2021, standing behind Europe and Central Asia, but exceeding the average of all other regions including high-income countries as well as the world's average. In particular, the share of goods trade in MENA GDP is more than twice the share for North America. In 2021, the MENA region exported more goods than it imported, exceeding the world's average share of goods exports in GDP, as well as the share for all regions except Europe and Central Asia, developing as well as developed ones. The share of goods exports in MENA GDP (27.59%) is more than twice the share for South Asia and triple the share for North America (Figure 2). Those bright figures are expected given the heavy reliance of the region on oil exports. Indeed, Reinert (2017) highlights that trade in goods is heavily influenced by regional factors, which is particularly relevant for the MENA region, where natural resource endowments and trade policies shape trade patterns.

However, the region's average masks the apparent heterogeneity in goods trade figures at the country level. Figure 3 shows that in 2021, although

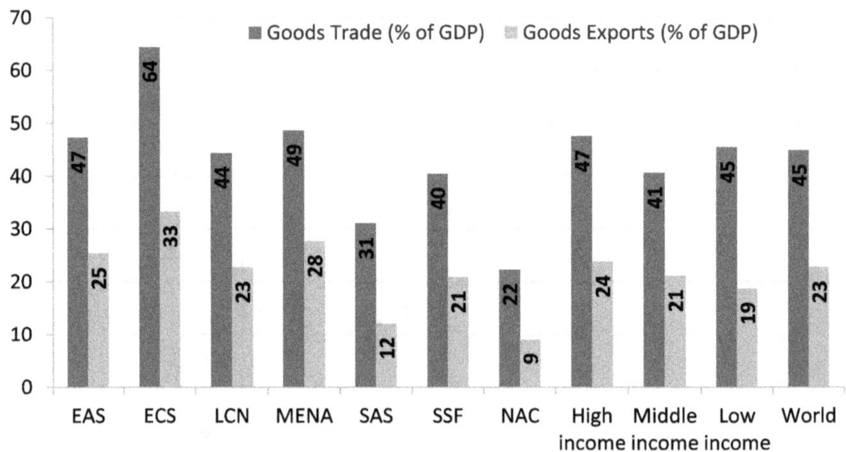

Figure 2 Goods trade as a percentage of GDP, 2021

Source: Authors' calculations from the World Bank, World Development Indicators database online, 2024.

Note: (i) Goods trade in GDP is calculated as the sum of goods imports and goods exports divided by GDP, all in current US$. Goods exports in GDP is calculated as the share of goods exports in GDP, all in current US$.

(ii) EAS: East Asia & Pacific; ECS: Europe & Central Asia; LCN: Latin America & Caribbean; MENA: Middle East & North Africa; SAS: South Asia; SSF: Sub-Saharan Africa; NAC: North America.

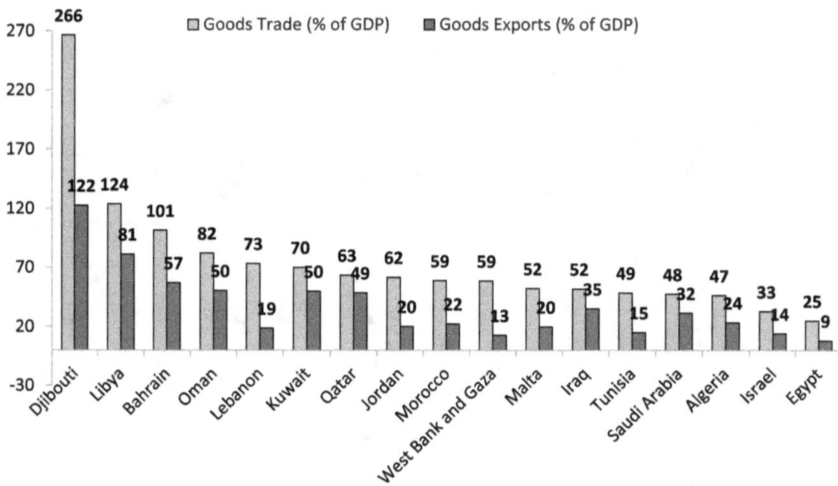

Figure 3 Goods trade as a percentage of GDP by country, 2021

Source: Authors' calculations from the World Bank, World Development Indicators database online, 2024.

Note: Goods trade in GDP is calculated as the sum of goods imports and goods exports divided by GDP, all in current US$. Goods exports in GDP is calculated as the share of goods exports in GDP, all in current US$.

most oil exporters are on the top in terms of the share of goods trade and exports in GDP, Djibouti, a non-oil-exporting country, ranks first in terms of goods trade and exports in GDP (266.32% and 122.48% respectively), with shares accounting for more than four times the regional averages. The most recent exports in Djibouti are led by Palm Oil ($169 M), Chlorides ($53 M), Sheep and Goats ($16.7 M), Dried Legumes ($10.2 M), and Industrial Fatty Acids, Oils and Alcohols ($8.66 M) (The Observatory of Economic Complexity, OEC (2021) https://oec.world/en/profile/country/dji). In addition, while GCC countries and other oil-exporting countries are net exporters, Djibouti seems to import more than it exports. It is also noteworthy that, while most oil exporters exceed the regional trade averages, the shares of goods trade and goods exports in the GDP of Saudi Arabia, the major oil exporter in the world, are below the region's average (47.58% and 31.6% respectively). Countries like Lebanon, Jordan, Morocco, and Malta show a share of goods trade in GDP above the region's average and are all net-importers of goods.

Trade in the MENA region has long been seen as interchangeable with trade in petroleum products, with two-thirds of MENA countries depending on the oil sector as the main source of earnings. Figure 4 shows that the share of oil

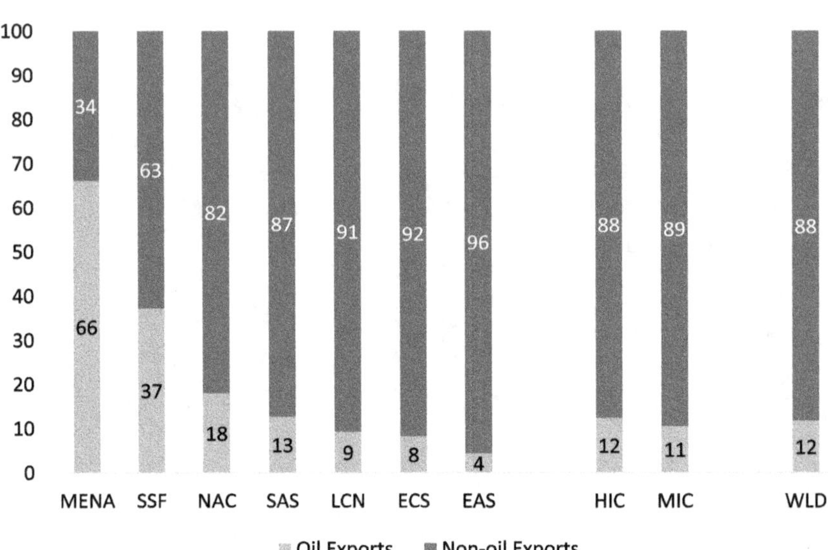

Figure 4 Oil v/s non-oil exports as a percentage of merchandise exports, 2021

Source: World Bank, World Development Indicators database online, 2024.

Note: EAS: East Asia & Pacific; ECS: Europe & Central Asia; LCN: Latin America & Caribbean; MENA: Middle East & North Africa; SAS: South Asia; SSF: Sub-Saharan Africa; NAC: North America.

exports in MENA merchandise exports is 66%, which is more than five times the world's average and almost double the average of developing regions like sub-Saharan Africa.

GCC countries expectedly show in 2021 the largest share of oil exports in total exports, reaching 94.63% for Kuwait, 84.40% for Qatar and 77.49% for Saudi Arabia. While the UAE is one of the major oil exporters with oil exports accounting for 70% of total merchandise exports, it stands behind major GCC exporting countries due to the deployed efforts to diversify its economy (Figure 5).

Therefore, as shown in Figure 5, the share of oil exports in total exports ranges from 65% to 95% in MENA oil-exporting countries, and oil revenues account for more than 60% of their GDP (Karam and Zaki, 2015). Heavy dependence on oil is a double-edged sword. While the region's abundant natural resources have fueled the region's rapid economic growth for decades, they have relentlessly exposed it to trade shocks and increased growth volatility over time. Consequently, recent years have seen governments embarking on ambitious economic diversification initiatives to decrease their dependence on oil.

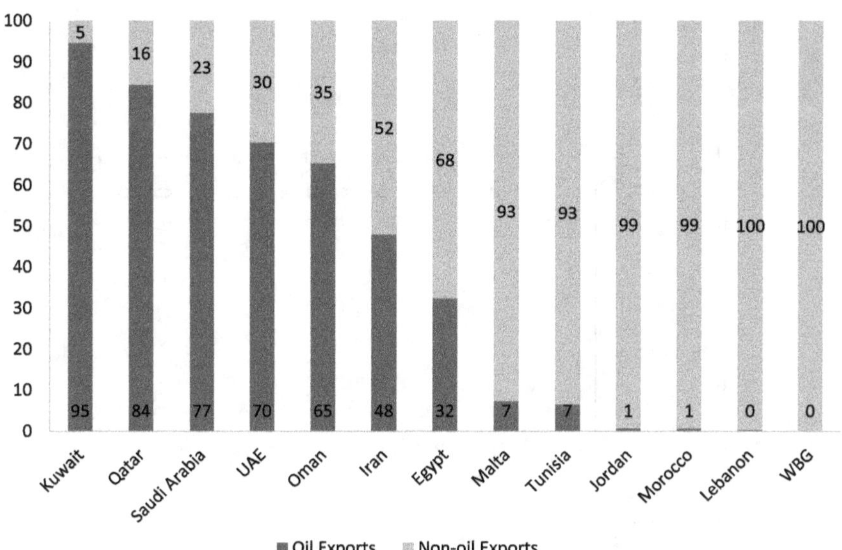

Figure 5 Oil v/s non-oil exports as a percentage of merchandise exports for selected MENA countries, 2021

Source: World Bank, World Development Indicators database online, 2024.
Note: UAE: United Arab Emirates; WBG: West Bank & Gaza.

An economy's vulnerability to external shocks mainly depends on export concentration in a limited number of products and trading partners. Columns 3 and 6 of Table 3 display the product export concentration index in 2000 and 2022 for MENA countries. The export concentration index shows to which degree exports of individual economies or of groups of economies are concentrated on a few products rather than being distributed in a more homogeneous manner among several products (UNCTAD). An index value closer to 1 indicates that exports are highly concentrated in a few products. An index value closer to 0 indicates that exports are more homogeneously distributed among a series of products. Columns 4 and 7 of Table 3 show the export diversification index in 2000 and 2022 for MENA countries. The export diversification index indicates to what extent the structure of exports by product of a given economy or group of economies differs from the world pattern (UNCTAD). The diversification index ranges between 0 and 1: a value of zero means the country's exports match the world average. Higher values indicate the country's dependence on a small number of products.

Table 3 shows that oil-exporting countries are more concentrated in their export products than oil-importing countries, and this finding seems to be persistent over time. Indeed, the export concentration index is higher for oil

Table 3 Export concentration and diversification indices in MENA countries: 2000 vs. 2022

	2000			2022		
	Number of products	**Concentration index**	**Diversification index**	**Number of products**	**Concentration index**	**Diversification index**
MENA oil exporters						
GCC countries						
Bahrain	189	0.409	0.788	225	0.332	0.705
Kuwait	183	0.618	0.829	243	0.276	0.619
Oman	177	0.801	0.784	242	0.292	0.639
Qatar	149	0.603	0.842	219	0.516	0.759
Saudi Arabia	246	0.664	0.8	251	0.592	0.751
UAE	254	0.464	0.656	259	0.294	0.529
Non-GCC countries						
Algeria	101	0.515	0.834	122	0.543	0.77
Iran	228	0.779	0.819	253	0.288	0.646
Iraq	77	0.974	0.85	174	0.907	0.849
Libya	80	0.763	0.822	93	0.759	0.807
Yemen	113	0.861	0.848	145	0.436	0.724

MENA oil importers

Djibouti	63	0.107	0.517	189	0.12	0.585
Egypt	224	0.212	0.635	232	0.178	0.559
Israel	211	0.312	0.592	216	0.176	0.491
Jordan	201	0.171	0.589	209	0.244	0.67
Lebanon	185	0.126	0.634	214	0.131	0.619
Malta	165	0.540	0.701	184	0.279	0.585
Morocco	201	0.176	0.726	229	0.212	0.695
Syria	150	0.62	0.783	219	0.166	0.653
Tunisia	190	0.207	0.669	226	0.143	0.506
WBG	135	0.178	0.609	157	0.163	0.684

Source: Constructed by the authors from UNCTAD data center https://unctadstat.unctad.org/datacentre/

Notes: (i) The export concentration index shows to which degree exports of individual economies or of groups of economies are concentrated on a few products rather than being distributed in a more homogeneous manner among several products (UNCTAD). An index value closer to 1 indicates that exports are highly concentrated in a few products. An index value closer to 0 indicates that exports are more homogeneously distributed among a series of products. (ii) The export diversification index indicates to what extent the structure of exports by product of a given economy or group of economies differs from the world pattern (UNCTAD). The diversification index ranges between 0 and 1: a value of zero means the country's exports match the world average. Higher values indicate the country's dependence on a small number of products. (iii) UAE: United Arab Emirates; WBG: West Bank & Gaza.

exporters than oil importers in 2000 and in 2022. In 2022, the more concentrated countries in their export products are Iraq, Yemen, Oman, Iran, and Libya with export concentration indices of 0.974, 0.861, 0.801, 0.779, and 0.763 respectively. Non-GCC oil-exporting countries appear to be less concentrated in export products than GGC countries in 2022. It is noteworthy that the export concentration index decreased for most countries between 2000 and 2022, mostly for oil-exporting countries, and particularly GGC countries among oil exporters, relatively to non-oil-exporting countries, highlighting the efforts deployed by the governments to decrease their heavy dependence on natural resources. Indeed, the index decreased significantly for oil exporters like Oman (from 0.801 to 0.292), Iran (from 0.779 to 0.288), Kuwait (from 0.618 to 0.276), and Yemen (from 0.861 to 0.436). One exception to that is Algeria that witnessed a mild increase in its index (from 0.515 to 0.543). Oil importers have seen an increase in their export concentration except for Egypt, Israel, Syria, and Tunisia.

The export diversification index tells a similar story; that is, oil exporters are generally less diversified than oil importers, and that oil exporters became more diversified over time. The United Arab Emirates (UAE) is the most diversified economy among oil exporters and, in 2022, becomes one of the most diversified MENA economies with an export diversification index of 0.529, standing slightly behind Israel (0.491) and Tunisia (0.506). The least diversified oil-exporting countries in 2000 were Iraq (0.85), Yemen (0.48), Qatar (0.842), Algeria (0.834), and Kuwait (0.829). Despite achieving some progress in product diversification, Iraq, Libya, Qatar, and Saudi Arabia are the least diversified oil exporters in 2020 with an export diversification index of 0.849, 0.807, 0.759, and 0.751 respectively. Among oil importers, Syria and Morocco are the least diversified, displaying values of the diversification index around 0.8, similar to most oil exporters. The same countries are on the top of the least diversified economies in 2022, although they have made some progress in this regard. According to Acharyya and Ganguly (2023), countries with less diversified exports tend to experience greater income inequality and vulnerability to external shocks. In the case of Morocco and Syria, their limited export base leads to the concentration of wealth and income among a few, such as those in primary sectors like agriculture (in Morocco) or oil (in Syria). Additionally, reliance on agricultural exports in Morocco means that climate change can significantly impact income levels, while dependence on oil in Syria makes it vulnerable to fluctuations in global oil prices. In both countries, the lack of diversification reflects constraints in education, skills development, and technological capabilities, hindering the shift to higher-quality exports that could promote broader economic opportunities and reduce inequality.

5.2 Trade in Services

Chanda (2017) emphasizes the growing importance of services trade in the global economy, a trend that is particularly relevant for MENA countries that are increasingly relying on services as part of their development strategies, to drive economic diversification, create jobs, and promote sustainable growth, away from traditional sectors like oil and gas. According to data from the World Development Indicators (WDI), the share of service value added in MENA GDP stands at 52.43% in 2021. Despite the fact that the production of services is a core activity in the MENA region, the share of services in MENA GDP is below the world's average (63.97%), the average for high-income countries (70%), as well as the average for developed regions like North America (76.58%) and Europe and Central Asia (64,14%). While the share of services in MENA GDP is almost comparable to middle-income countries (52.95%), it exceeds the figure for South Asia (48.87%) and for developing regions like sub-Saharan Africa (47.76%) as well as the average for low-income countries (36.15%).

Although the share of service value added in GDP appears to be positively linked to countries' income level, standing at 70% for high-income countries, against 53% and 36%, respectively, in middle- and low-income countries, the picture looks different for MENA countries, highlighting significant differences existing between income groups as well as within the same group. Indeed, WDI data show that high-income countries like Qatar, the UAE, Oman, Saudi Arabia, and Bahrain have a share of service value added in GDP below the region's average, while in Malta and Israel, service value added accounts for 78% and 72% of GDP, respectively, exceeding by far the region's average. In addition, in some low- and middle-income countries, the share of services in GDP exceeds the region's average as well as the same share for high-income countries in the region, such as in Lebanon (94%), Djibouti (75%), Tunisia, Jordan, and West Bank and Gaza (around 60%). By contrast, other countries in the same income group show a share of service value added in GDP below the regional average, such as Libya (26%), Iraq, and Syria (43%).

Although the previous figures show that the service sector is a core activity in the MENA region, Figure 6 shows that trade in services as percentage of GDP only accounts for 6.68% of MENA GDP. However, and surprisingly, the share of service trade in MENA GDP exceeds the world's average (12.19%), the average for high-income countries (15.4%), as well as the average of all other regions, developed and developing ones, except Europe and Central Asia (23.89%). Indeed, Figure 7 shows that this favorable standing of the MENA region is mainly due to countries like Malta where service trade accounted for

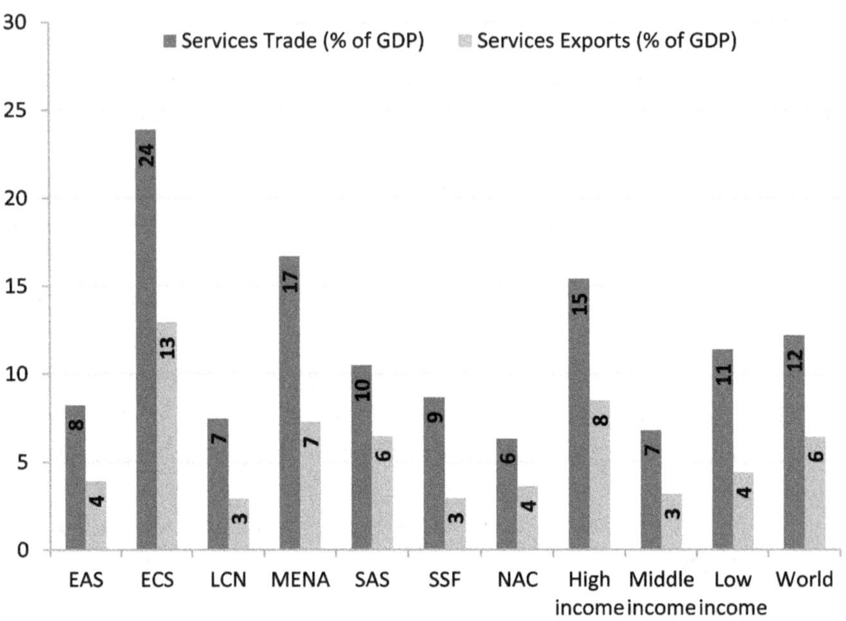

Figure 6 Services trade as a percentage of GDP, 2021

Source: Authors' calculations from the World Bank, World Development Indicators database online, 2024.

Note: (i) Trade in services is the sum of service exports and imports divided by the value of GDP, all in current U.S. dollars (data available). Services exports in GDP is calculated as the share of services exports in GDP, all in current US$.
(ii) EAS: East Asia & Pacific; ECS: Europe & Central Asia; LCN: Latin America & Caribbean; MENA: Middle East & North Africa; SAS: South Asia; SSF: Sub-Saharan Africa; NAC: North America.

215.87% of GDP, Bahrain, Djibouti, and Lebanon where the share of service trade in GDP is almost triple the region's average (60.62%, 48.04%, and 45.77% respectively). Not only Malta displays the highest figure relatively to all MENA countries, but also this figure is at least 3.5 times the share of the second standing country which is Djibouti. A closer look to Figure 7 reveals significant differences between countries within the same income group. For instance, in high-income countries other than Malta and Bahrain, such as Qatar, Israel, and Kuwait, trade in services accounts for 22–29% of GDP, which is half the figure for Bahrain, and almost one-seventh the figure for Malta. At the same time, high-income countries such as Oman and Saudi Arabia fall behind the region's average (12.95% and 9.56% respectively). Similarly, while Djibouti and Lebanon stand far from their peers with shares being more than double the regional average, other low- and middle-income countries, like Libya, Tunisia,

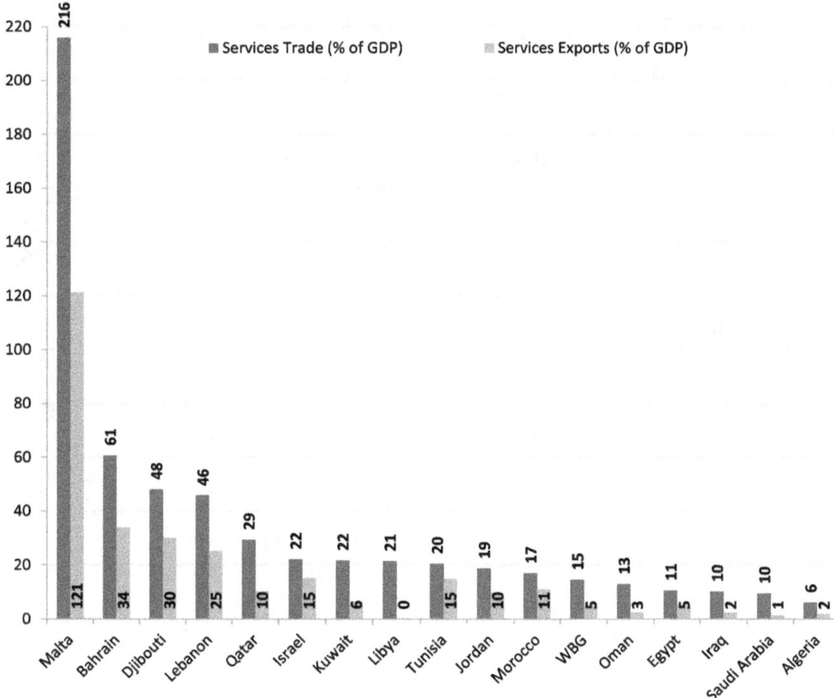

Figure 7 Services trade as a percentage of GDP by country, 2021

Source: Authors' calculations from the World Bank, World Development Indicators database online, 2024.

Note: (i) Trade in services is the sum of service exports and imports divided by the value of GDP, all in current U.S. dollars (data available). Services exports in GDP is calculated as the share of services exports in GDP, all in current US$.
(ii) WBG: West Bank and Gaza.

Jordan, and Morocco, exhibit a share of service trade in GDP that beats the region's average but is half the share of Djibouti and Lebanon. On the other hand, low- and middle-income countries such as West Bank and Gaza, Egypt, Iraq, and Algeria fall behind the regional average, and Algeria ranks last among MENA countries with a share of service trade in GDP of 6.20%. At the sectoral level, Table 4 shows that financial services dominate MENA exports of services (in both oil-rich and oil-poor countries), followed by insurance, and government services (for more details, see Table A.2 in the appendix).

A closer look at Figure 6 reveals that while high-income countries and developed regions are net exporters of services, the MENA region is a net importer of services, just like middle- and low-income countries, and other developing regions such as Latin America and the Caribbean and sub-Saharan

Table 4 Trade in services – top sector – 2021 (%)

MENA oil exporters

GCC countries		
Bahrain	Telecommunications, computer, and information services	58.6
Kuwait	Government goods and services	46.1
Oman	Insurance and pension services	35.9
Qatar	Transport	61.6
Saudi Arabia	Financial services	37.1
UAE	Financial services	33.8
Non-GCC countries		
Algeria	Maintenance and repair services	58.9
Iran	Financial services	59.2
Iraq	Financial services	37.9
Libya	Telecommunications, computer, and information services	30.8
Yemen	Travel	36.6
MENA oil importers		
Djibouti	Insurance and pension services	56.7
Egypt	Financial services	40.6
Israel	Government goods and services	37.0
Jordan	Financial services	61.2
Lebanon	Financial services	53.6
Malta	Other	53.2
Morocco	Financial services	24.9
Syria	Financial services	84.4
Tunisia	Financial services	35.0
Palestine	Travel	72.2

Source: Authors' own elaboration using the International Trade Center database. All data are those of 2021 except for Bahrain (2020), Iran (2019), Libya (2020), Yemen (2020), Israel (2020), and Syria (2010). For more details, see Table A2.

Africa. Indeed, service exports only account for 7.26% of MENA GDP in 2021, although this share beats the world's average as well as the average for other regions except Europe and Central Asia (12.93%), and all income groups except high-income countries (8.47%). However, not all MENA countries are net importers of services. Figure 7 shows that the following countries are net exporters of services: Malta, Djibouti, Bahrain, Lebanon, Israel, Tunisia, Jordan, and Morocco. In 2021, Malta exhibited the largest share of service exports in GDP (121.35%), which is at least 3.5 times higher than the other major service exporters such as Bahrain (33.81%), Djibouti (29.93%), and Lebanon (25.28%). Malta is a hub for financial services, and has developed a strong regulatory framework to attract international financial institutions. Additionally, it is popular for tourism and business services (legal, accounting, consulting services), and is a leading center for online gaming and iGaming services, with many international gaming companies operating from there. Bahrain is a major exporter of financial services, tourism, business services, logistics and transportation services, and Djibouti is known for port and logistics services, financial services, and tourism. Lebanon is a major exporter of IT services and education services, in addition to tourism and financial services. As expected, GGC countries, excluding Bahrain and Qatar, and non-GCC oil exporters display a modest share of service exports in GDP, below the regional average, with the lowest figures being for Saudi Arabia (1.18%), Algeria (1.97%), and Oman (2.53%).

Despite the low share of service trade in GDP and the fact that the MENA region is a net importer of services, as highlighted from the comparison of panels (a) and (c) from Figure 8, it is noteworthy that exports and imports of services have both increased in the MENA region since 2005, before declining sharply in 2020–2021 due to the COVID-19 pandemic. In fact, the evolution over the years of both MENA service exports and imports are comparable to the evolution of world service exports and imports, all bouncing back after the pandemic. However, the growth of MENA exports and imports of services has not kept pace with the growth of world service exports and imports post-pandemic, reflecting losses in market shares of MENA countries (Figure 8). Indeed, while world service exports and imports have reached record levels after the pandemic, MENA service exports only hit the pre-pandemic level in 2022, while MENA service imports surpass the pre-pandemic import level. This observation points to a loss of competitiveness of MENA exporters in key services activities. For instance, Lebanon's financial sector, once a regional hub, has faced significant challenges due to political instability and an ongoing economic crisis. Improvements in infrastructure and service efficiency in Kenya and Ethiopia have affected Djibouti's competitiveness in logistics and transportation services. MENA's tourism exports post-pandemic have seen slower recoveries than other countries such as Greece and Turkey, drawing visitors away from MENA destinations.

As shown in the preceding analysis of trade flows, there are clear asymmetries in trade performance and integration across MENA countries. One important institutional factor contributing to these differences is WTO membership, which significantly shapes trade dynamics in the region by promoting

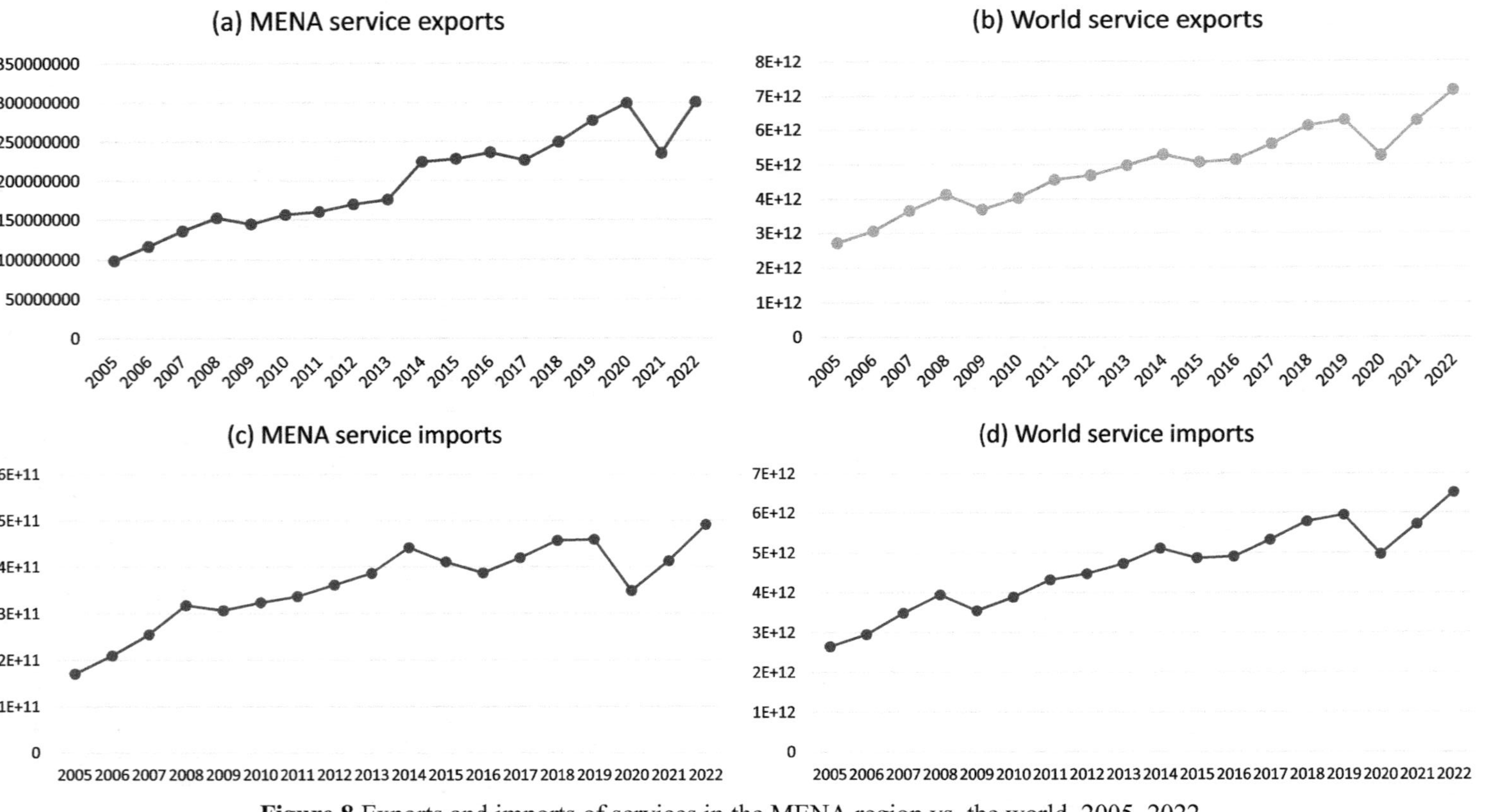

Figure 8 Exports and imports of services in the MENA region vs. the world, 2005–2022

Source: Authors' calculations from the World Bank, World Development Indicators database online, 2024 and from Trade Map, International Trade Center.

Note: Trade values are in current US dollars.

adherence to common standards, transparency, and predictable dispute settlement mechanisms. Among the MENA countries, thirteen are members of the WTO, while seven – namely Algeria, Iran, Iraq, Lebanon, Libya, Palestine, Syria, and Yemen – are not. This uneven membership landscape creates disparities in trade governance across the region. Non-WTO members often follow less transparent and more unpredictable trade policies, which can raise transaction costs and create uncertainty for neighboring countries. These differences hinder effective policy coordination and pose challenges to deeper bilateral and regional trade integration efforts. Having described MENA trade patterns, we now shift our focus to discussing MENA trading partners.

5.3 Concentration of Trade Partners

Historical, political, and economic factors shape the concentration of trading partners in the MENA region. First, historical factors include colonial ties and ancient trade routes. Post-independence, MENA countries continued to have strong trade ties with their former colonizers. To illustrate, Algeria, Morocco, and Tunisia still maintain strong trade ties with France, while Kuwait and Egypt sustain solid links with the United Kingdom. Moreover, many MENA countries entered into free trade agreements with their former colonizers. In particular, the European Union has various agreements with MENA countries that reflect historical colonial connections. Ancient trade routes, such as the Silk Road and spice routes, that historically facilitated trade between the MENA region, Asia, and Europe, also continue to influence MENA's current trade ties. In addition, trade with sub-Saharan Africa has much historical significance, particularly for both North African and Gulf countries. Trans-Saharan trade routes once connected cities such as Tripoli, Fez, and Cairo, enabling the exchange of gold, salt, ivory and textiles. More recently, economic ties between MENA and sub-Saharan Africa have expanded, especially as Gulf countries like Saudi Arabia, the UAE, and Qatar have increased investment and trade with sub-Saharan economies in agriculture, infrastructure, telecommunications, and other. Similarly, North African countries such as Morocco and Egypt have strengthened south–south cooperation with West and Central African nations, particularly in banking, construction, and pharmaceuticals. These deep-rooted and evolving ties underscore the multidirectional nature of the MENA region's trade relations.

Political instability and conflicts in the MENA region have profound implications for trade relationships as well. For example, the sanctions on Iran and Syria imposed by major global powers have increased the reliance of both countries on trading partners within the region and have expanded collaboration with other countries such as Russia and China. The conflict in Yemen has affected Saudi Arabia's trade partners by impacting shipping routes through the Red Sea. The blockade and ongoing conflict Iraq's trade relationships have been affected by years of conflict and political instability. The rise and fall of ISIS and ongoing security issues have disrupted trade routes and production. The 2017 blockade of Qatar by Saudi Arabia, the UAE, Bahrain, and Egypt led to countries like Turkey and Iran stepping in to fill the gap left by the blockading countries, leading to shifts in trade patterns and new trade relationships.

Oil wealth, market size, and economic diversification represent the main economic factors that shape the concentration of trade partners for MENA countries. Indeed, GCC countries such as Saudi Arabia, the UAE, Kuwait, and Qatar possess some of the world's largest oil and natural gas reserves, making them crucial suppliers in the global energy market. Major oil importers, including the United States, China, Japan, and European countries, are among their key trading partners. Oil wealth also enables these countries to form strategic alliances with major global powers. For instance, the United States has strong ties with Saudi Arabia due to its role as a major oil supplier. Moreover, the market size of a country plays an important role in attracting trading partners. Highly populated countries with large markets like Egypt import a wide range of goods to meet domestic needs, making them attractive as trading partners. Finally, economic diversification affects the choice of trading partners. To illustrate, countries like the UAE, Saudi Arabia, and Qatar have started to diversify their economies by investing in sectors such as tourism, finance, technology, and renewable energy, which is attracting a broader range of trade partners interested in these emerging industries. Additionally, diversified economies are more likely to enter into various trade agreements and regional integrations. Examples include Jordan and Morocco's bilateral trade agreements with the United States, as well as EU-MED FTA between the European Union and Mediterranean countries. It is also noteworthy that MENA countries put in substantial efforts to promote intra-regional trade and reduce dependence on external partners, with the establishment of regional trade agreements, such as the GCC, Agadir Agreement, and GAFTA.

Figure 9 displays the evolution in export partner shares (panels (a) and (b)) and import partner shares (panels (c) and (d)) of the MENA region between 1990 and 2021. On the one hand, panels (a) and (b) of Figure 9 show that MENA market is still the main export destination for MENA countries, with a deeper integration within the region highlighted by an increase in the export share with the MENA region from 5.43% to 15.74% between 1990 and 2021. The main export markets beyond the region itself are Europe & Central Asia, East Asia & Pacific, and South Asia. Export shares also increased substantially with these

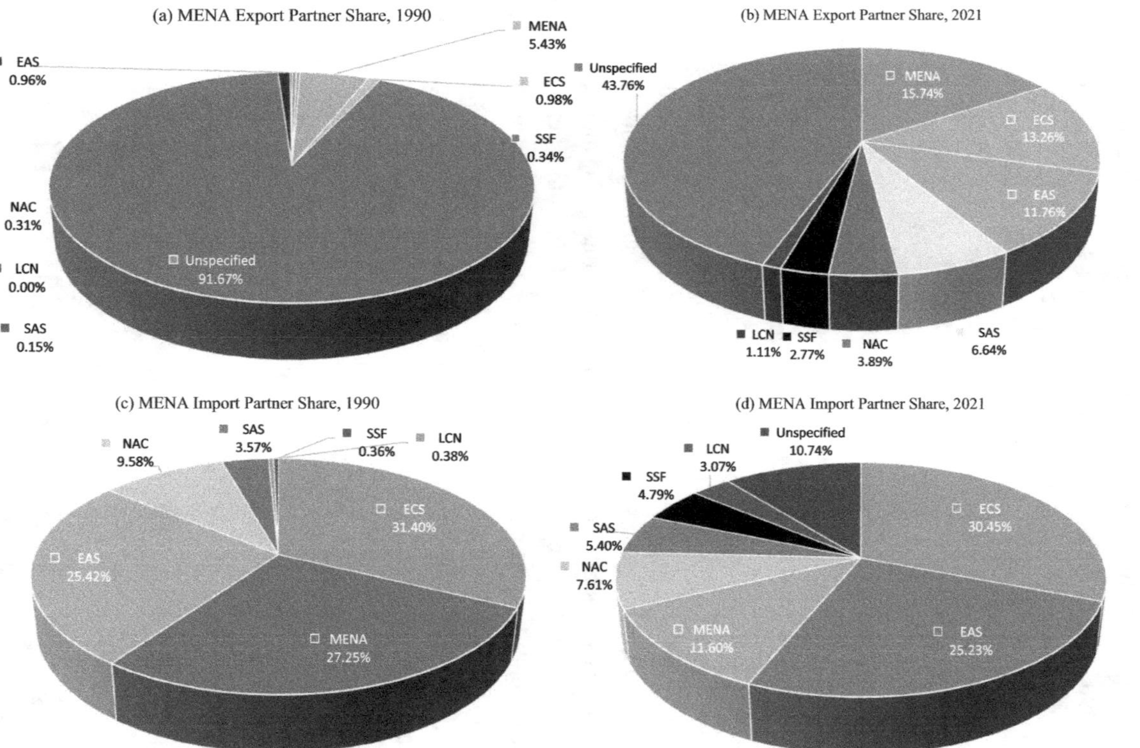

Figure 9 MENA export and import partner shares, 2021

Source: World Integrated Trade Solution (WITS), the World Bank.

Note: (i) Export and Import Partner Share is the share of total merchandise trade (export or import) accounted for by the partner in a given year (WITS).
(ii) EAS: East Asia & Pacific; ECS: Europe & Central Asia; LCN: Latin America & Caribbean; MENA: Middle East & North Africa; SAS: South Asia; SSF: Sub-Saharan Africa; NAC: North America.

regions: Europe & Central Asia (from 0.98% to 13.26%), East Asia & Pacific (from 0.96% to 11.76%), and South Asia (from 0.15% to 6.64%).

On the other hand, panels (c) and (d) of Figure 9 show that Europe & Central Asia and East Asia & Pacific represent, since 1990, the main import partners for the MENA region. While MENA countries relied heavily on the region itself for their imports in 1990, with an import share of 27.25%, the same share fell to 11.6% in 2021, highlighting the fact that MENA countries have turned toward other import partners from outside the region, especially from South Asia, sub-Saharan Africa, Latin America, and Caribbean that exhibited low or almost inexistent import shares in 1990.

6 Trade and Firm Dynamics: A Micro Approach

After examining the trade patterns of the MENA at the macroeconomic level, it is important to analyze trade from the firms' perspective. The "New-New Trade theory" (Melitz, 2003) has shown that only the most productive firms are able to bear the sunk cost of exports and serve both the foreign and the domestic markets. Less productive firms are able to produce only for the domestic market and the least productive ones will exit from it. Figure 10 shows that the share of exporting firms in the MENA region is higher than other ones. Yet, this result must be analyzed with caution as the lion share of firm export oil and other refined products. However, non-oil-exporting firms are much lower, which affects export diversification and the likelihood of integration into global value chains. In addition, the share of firms that use imported materials and inputs is always higher than exporting firms but rather comparable to other emerging and developing regions. Thus, two-way traders (being a proxy of GVC integration) represent a minority (Dovis and Zaki, 2020).

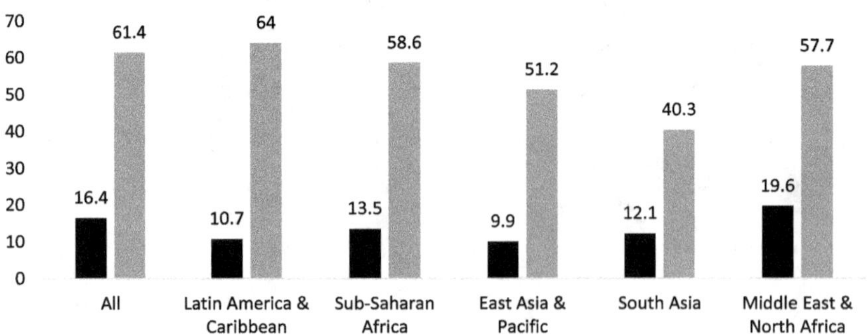

Figure 10 Percent of firms trading – by region

Source: Authors' own elaboration using the World Bank Enterprise Survey.

When the firm size is considered, Table 5 shows that the highest share of exporting firms belongs to the category of large ones. Indeed, Jaud and Freund (2015) show that the MENA region is characterized by the dominance of some superstars who export. However, there is a significant heterogeneity across the region as the share of large exporting firms ranges between 16% in Egypt and 74% in Tunisia. These figures are much higher for importing firms and for all sizes as it is shown in the right panel of Table 5. Moreover, small exporters are still underrepresented in trade relations as their share does not exceed 20% in most of the countries, with the exception of Tunisia (40%). This result is of particular importance as helping SMEs to export and integrate regional and global value chains should be a development priority given the importance of SMEs in developing countries and their ability to generate jobs.

At the sectoral level, there is also a large variation across different countries, with most of the exporting firms in the manufacturing sector, except for Djibouti and Yemen (see Table 6). At a more detailed level, the WBES dataset shows that most of these firms belong to a few sectors especially oil and its refineries, chemical products, textile and ready-made garments, processed food, and only a handful of firms in high-tech sectors (such as the automotive industry in Morocco).

Table 5 Percent of firms trading – by size and country

		Exporting directly or indirectly (at least 10% of sales)			Using material inputs and/or supplies of foreign origin		
		Small (5–19)	**Medium (20–99)**	**Large (100+)**	**Small (5–19)**	**Medium (20–99)**	**Large (100+)**
Djibouti	2013	21	15.3	53.4	74.5	64	n.a.
Egypt	2020	5.2	13.4	16	29.5	38.9	41.6
Iraq	2022	4.3	7.5	16.1	42.8	61.6	85.9
Jordan	2019	12.2	46.5	53	79.5	92.6	97.5
Lebanon	2019	18.6	34.5	23.1	54.4	77.6	68.3
Malta	2019	18.2	23	66.7	80.7	90	100
Morocco	2023	23.1	18.1	41.2	53.2	39.6	48.2
Saudi Arabia	2022	14.8	21.1	18.8	11.8	45.8	66.6
Tunisia	2020	40.1	16.5	74.3	69.2	45.5	86.3
Palestine	2023	16.4	23.2	14.5	54.6	77.3	38.7
Yemen, Rep.	2013	11.2	10	33.4	34.3	36.8	84.9

Source: Authors' own elaboration using the World Bank Enterprise Survey.

Table 6 Percent of firms exporting directly or indirectly (at least
10% of sales) – by sector and country

		Manufacturing	**Services**
Djibouti	2013	13.8	23.3
Egypt	2020	8.7	6.7
Iraq	2022	9.9	3.7
Israel	2013	24.9	11.4
Jordan	2019	54.8	14.2
Lebanon	2019	39.8	15.1
Malta	2019	27.7	23.7
Morocco	2023	27.3	19.2
Saudi Arabia	2022	24.9	15.1
Tunisia	2020	52.8	13.1
West Bank and Gaza	2023	42.8	1.4
Yemen	2013	9.5	13.7

Source: Authors' own elaboration using the World Bank Enterprise Survey.

To explain the patterns of firms trading behavior in MENA countries, it is important to examine the characteristics of the investment climate (Dollar et al., 2004 and Kinda, 2009). Figure 11 shows indeed that most of the firms in the MENA region identify corruption, political instability, customs and trade regulations, and tax rates as a major constraint to their business. This in line with the findings of Aboushady and Zaki (2019) who show that investment climate matters for both the extensive (likelihood of exporting) and the intensive (quantity of exports) margins of exports for Egypt. They argue that the main obstacles to increasing the limited number of exporters and/or the quantity of exports are those connected to politics, macroeconomics, institutions, and competitiveness. Tax payments and competition from the informal sector influence a firm's decision to become an exporter, while political unrest and corruption have an impact on the volume of exports. Access to finance affects both margins. This is why serious and deep reforms of the investment climate are crucial to improve the performance of exporting firms in MENA countries. The literature has also shown that another major constraint for firms pertains to political connections as more politically connected firms are more able to protect themselves and to better integrate the exporting market or GVC (Kruz et al., 2021 and Aboushady and Zaki, 2025). Obviously, to specialize into more complex and less traditional sectors, the MENA region needs better institutions (property rights, enforcement of contracts, less corruption, etc.) as it will be shown later.

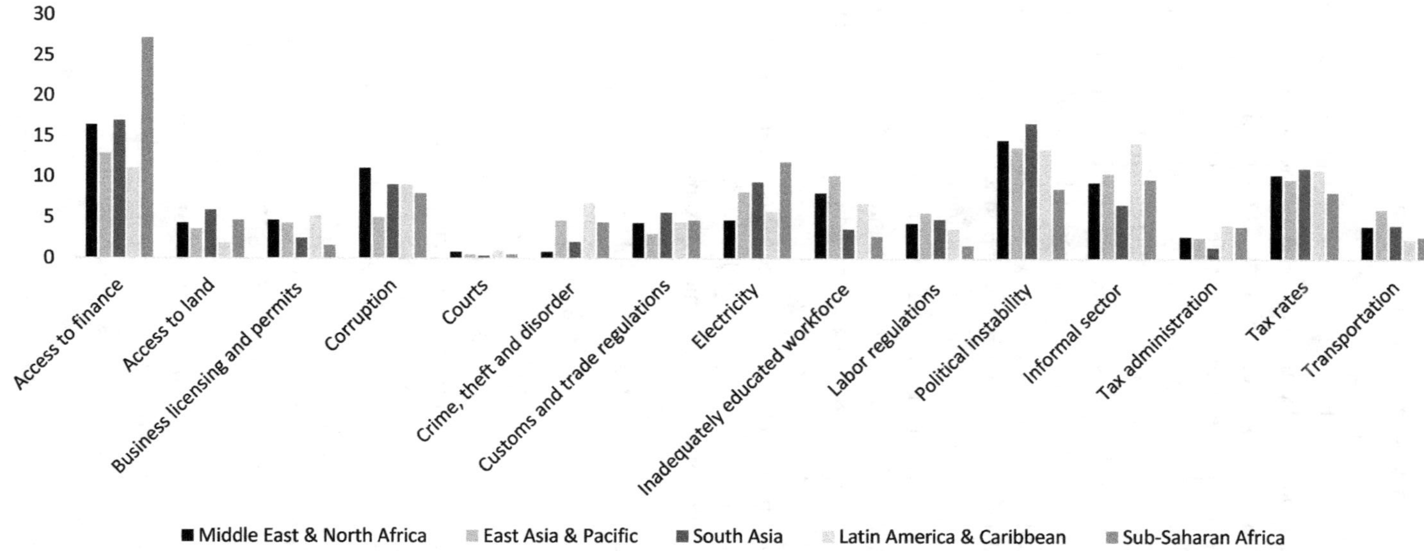

Figure 11 Firms identifying each barrier as a major constraint – average by region

Source: Authors' own elaboration using the World Bank Enterprise Survey.

Another key determinant of the firms' performance in the MENA region is digitalization. Indeed, the Schumpeterian growth theory can help understand how digital technologies can affect firms. Innovations result from entrepreneurial investments that are motivated by the prospects of monopoly rents (Aghion, 2002). This will lead to the notion of creative destruction, which shows the process by which new innovations replace older technologies. In this context, only the most productive firms will bear the disruptions caused by technological innovations, and thus will survive and be able to perform better. At the empirical level, Bellakhal and Mouelhi (2023) show that, for Tunisia, there is a positive association between digitalization and firms' performance. In the same vein, for Egypt and Jordan, Zaki (2023) shows that, while, in Egypt, digitalization is associated with better outcomes at the labor market level (as more women, less unpaid workers and more workers with permanent contract), less robust results are obtained for sales and exports. Yet, for sales, the use of the Internet is significant in both Egypt and Jordan. In terms of exports, self-built websites for payments in Egypt and using Internet in Jordan are significant. Helping firm to become more and better digitalized is crucial to survive and better integrate into the global economy.

These macro and micro features of trade in the MENA region are primarily due to several dimensions related to trade policy and to some structural characteristics of MENA countries. The next section thoroughly examines these points.

7 Potential Explanations of Trade Patterns

7.1 Trade Policies

Distortionary policies are counterproductive as they affect firms' performance. Anderson and van Wincoop (2004) argue that "trade costs are large, even aside from trade policy barriers and even between apparently highly integrated economies" (p. 691). Such trade costs may be decomposed in four categories (Zaki, 2017). The first component includes transaction costs that are related to transport (including distance) and insurance of traded goods. The second one pertains to costs induced by trade policies associated with tariff and nontariff measures (such as quotas, SPS, and TBT). The third one includes local distribution costs from foreign producers to final user in the domestic country that are affected by the quality of infrastructure. Finally, the fourth type of costs is due to administrative barriers or red tape costs that are related to trade facilitation. Against this background, trade policies are key in understanding the trade patterns of the MENA region. While MENA countries are part of different trade agreements and liberalized their trade to a certain extent, a lot of nontariff measures represent a large impediment to exports, imports, and thus GVC integration.

7.1.1 Tariffs

Despite a significant bilateral or multilateral liberalization, MENA countries still have on average high tariffs. The latter can affect imported inputs and foreign technology (Goldberg et al., 2010 and Luong, 2011), firms' participation in trade (Bas, 2012), and firms' productivity (Amiti and Konings, 2007). Indeed, firm competitiveness is a function of the cost and quality of the inputs to which firms have access. Yet, if imported goods are final or consumption goods, the consumer bears the cost of tariffs. Figure 12 shows that tariffs of the manufacturing sector in the MENA region are heterogeneous, ranging from almost 3% in Israel to 20% in Algeria and Iran. In addition, all the countries are more protectionist in the primary sector than in the manufacturing one with Egypt having the highest simple Most Favored Nation tariff at 40%.

7.1.2 Nontariff Measures

In addition to tariffs, MENA countries impose and face a lot of nontariff measures. NTMs are generally defined "as policy measures other than ordinary customs tariffs that can potentially have an economic effect on international trade in goods, changing quantities traded, or prices or both" (UNCTAD website). Moreover, NTMs are heterogeneous and have different advantages and disadvantages. On their heterogeneity, while the UNCTAD identifies sixteen chapters of NTMs, some of them are technical and related to the characteristics of the products (including sanitary and phytosanitary (SPS)

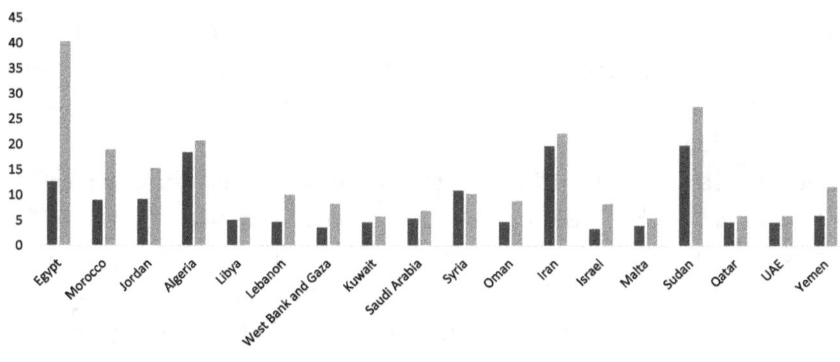

Figure 12 Tariff – by sector and country (2020)

Source: Authors' own elaboration using the World Development Indicators. Data for Egypt is for 2019, West Bank and Gaza, Israel and Yemen for 2017.

measures and technical barriers to trade (TBT)) and others are nontechnical and related to price or quantity restrictions (including contingent trade measures, quantitative restrictions, price controls, and finance measures).

Among the advantages of NTMs, one can cite mainly two (Bouet et al., 2020). First, they can help protect nascent and infant industries. Second, they can be used to protect human, animal, or plant life or health (such as the SPS or TBT measures) if they are scientifically justified and formally notified at the WTO.

However, their disadvantages are more numerous. First, they represent a distortion on the market as they can affect prices, quantities, access to varieties, and thus the consumer welfare.

Second, they are less transparent than tariffs and can be imposed for non-economic purposes (Kruse et al., 2021 and Ruckteschler et al., 2022). Indeed, for Egypt, Diwan et al. (2020) argue that NTMs increased with the gradual elimination of tariffs. Moreover, Eibl and Malik (2016) show that sectors characterized with politically connected firms experienced the imposition of more NTMs. In Morocco, similar results are found by Ruckteschler et al. (2022), who argue that politically connected sectors witnessed a rise in TBT. In Tunisia, firms connected to the Ben Ali family experienced higher NTMs after the implementation of the EU Association agreement (Kruse et al., 2021). Clearly, in these cases, NTMs can become more discriminatory.

Third, they negatively affect both the extensive (the probability of exporting) and the intensive margins (the quantity exported by firms) of exports. Indeed, El-Enbaby et al. (2016) and Kamal and Zaki (2018) show that SPS and TBT respectively negatively affect Egyptian exporters. They represent a fixed cost that affects more the extensive margin than the intensive one.

Table 7 analyzes the different NTMs imposed by MENA countries where most of the countries impose SPS, TBT, antidumping, or countervailing measures. While Gulf countries (Saudi Arabia, Bahrain, and UAE followed by Qatar and Oman) use heavily SPS and TBT measures, Egypt and Morocco rely also on TBT and antidumping ones.

Generally, SPS measures allow countries to protect human, animal, or plant life or health and must be based on science and imposed in an unarbitrary way. The same applies to TBT that are not, so far, used by MENA countries. As per antidumping measures, the literature shows that the latter are associated with three effects. First, the destruction effect refers to the fact that antidumping duties increase the price of imported goods, which reduces imports. The "investigation effect" refers to the case where the initiation of the antidumping investigation could have an impact on trade, even if tariff imposition is rejected (Prusa, 2001). Finally, the diversion effect is associated to a diversion of imports from countries concerned by the antidumping measures to non-concerned countries.

Table 7 Nontariff measures – by type (2010–2024)

	SPS	TBT	ADP	CV	SG	SSG	QR	TRQ
Egypt	97	314	52	8	11	–	–	–
Morocco	55	15	17	–	8	–	–	–
Tunisia	3	2	–	–	4	–	–	–
Bahrain, Kingdom of	168	464	–	–	4	–	–	–
Israel	1	888	17	–	1	–	–	–
Jordan	21	40	–	–	6	–	–	–
Kuwait, the State of	117	569	–	–	3	–	–	–
Oman	87	380	–	–	4	–	–	–
Qatar	124	457	–	–	3	–	–	–
Saudi Arabia, Kingdom of	471	1123	11	–	4	–	–	–
United Arab Emirates	235	503	–	–	4	–	–	–
Yemen	62	215	–	–	–	–	–	–
Middle East	1286	4639	28	–	29	–	–	–
Africa	891	5014	96	8	42	–	36	–
Europe	1099	2185	340	45	35	72	65	2
Least-developed countries	580	3531	1	–	11	–	50	–
North America	2548	2146	595	254	5	117	138	–
South and Central America and the Caribbean	3519	3325	519	16	28	17	116	–
Grand Total	14036	21725	2840	409	253	192	1234	6

Source: World Trade Organization I-TIP online dataset.
Notes: This table includes both measures initiated and enforced. Anti dumping [ADP], Countervailing [CV], Quantitative Restrictions [QR], Safeguards [SG], Sanitary and Phytosanitary [SPS], Special Safeguards [SSG], Technical Barriers to Trade [TBT], Tariff-rate quotas [TRQ], Export Subsidies [XS]

It is important to note that NTMs are not solely imposed by MENA countries as their main trade partners (the EU and the USA) use SPS and TBT in more extensive way. This is why several products, in case they do not comply with such standards, can be rejected at the border. Obviously, this will require, first, more investment and more programs by governments to help firms comply with stringent measures. Second, imposing countries must notify such measures in a more transparent way. Third, mutual recognition agreements (MRA) have also been an effective tool in reducing the negative impact of NTM and promoting trade. While MRAs are not frequently included in MENA's trade agreements, a few examples can be cited. For instance, in some EU association agreements (especially the one with Israel), one can find some MRAs. At the intra-MENA level, Egypt and Saudi Arabia have signed an agreement for the mutual recognition of authorized economic operator programs.[11] Clearly, such agreements are important, especially in the presence of a lot of NTMs. For instance, in the case of the mutual recognition arrangement established by Mexico with Canada and the United States in the electronics sector, Blyde (2023) finds that the latter led to an increase in the exports of the products associated with the agreement by around 23%. In a similar line of thought, Jang (2018), using data on MRAs in thirty-four countries and twenty-two manufacturing sectors between 1995 and 2009 shows that MRAs promote trade in member countries, especially for countries with a low technology level.

7.1.3 Trade Agreements

MENA countries signed different trade agreements ranging from the Pan Arab Free Trade Agreement (twenty-two Arab countries), to the Arab Maghreb Union (Algeria, Libya, Mauritania, Morocco, and Tunisia), Agadir Agreement (Egypt, Jordan, Tunisia, and Morocco), and Bilateral Associations with the EU (Algeria, Libya, Lebanon, Egypt, Jordan, Israel, Tunisia, Palestine, and Morocco), among others (see Table 8). These agreements are characterized by four main points. First, they focus primarily on tariff reduction, with weak reference to nontariff measures and services. Second, they do not cover broader policies that go beyond trade objectives. Thus, one can argue that most of these agreements are rather shallow. Indeed, the literature distinguishes between shallow and deep agreements. While the former focus on tariff removal, the latter go beyond this in a horizontal and a vertical way. The horizontal depth refers to the cases where a trade agreement includes different areas other than tariffs (the environment, services, nontariff measures, mobility of factors of production, industrial policy, or other social dimensions, etc.). The vertical depth refers, among others, to the legal enforceability of different provisions (Mattoo et al., 2020). Based on the two criteria, the MENA region is characterized by shallow agreements as most of them are limited to trade liberalization and they include a handful of provisions that are legally enforceable. Figure 13 shows that the average number of legally enforceable policy areas is generally

---

[11] https://www.sis.gov.eg/Story/202407/Egypt%2C-Saudi-Arabia-sign-agreement-for-mutual-rec ognition-of-authorized-economic-operator-programs#:~:text=Thursday%D8%8C%2005% 20December%202024%20%2D%2011:41%20AM&text=Deputy%20Minister%20of% 20Finance%20and,widespread%20adoption%20across%20various%20sectors.

Table 8 List of bilateral and regional agreements

Agreement	Year	Type
AfCFTA	2021	FTA
Agadir	2005	RTA
AMU	1989	EIA
COMESA	1994	CU
EC-Algeria	2005	FTA
EC-Egypt	2004	FTA
EC-Jordan	2002	FTA
EC-Lebanon	2003	FTA
EC-Israel	2000	FTA
EFTA-Israel	1993	FTA
US-Israel	1985	FTA
Canada – Israel	1997	FTA
Israel – Mexico	2000	FTA
Turkey – Israel	1997	FTA
EC-Morocco	2000	FTA
EC-Palestinian Authority	1997	FTA
EC-Syria	1977	FTA
EC-Tunisia	1998	FTA
GCC	2003	CU
PAFTA	1998	FTA
US-Bahrain	2006	FTA & EIA
US-Jordan	2001	FTA & EIA
US-Morocco	2006	FTA & EIA
US-Oman	2009	FTA & EIA
Canada–Jordan	2012	FTA
Gulf Cooperation Council (GCC)–Singapore	2013	FTA & EIA
Jordan–Singapore	2005	FTA & EIA
EFTA–Egypt	2007	FTA
EFTA–Jordan	2002	FTA
EFTA–Lebanon	2007	FTA
EFTA–Morocco	1999	FTA
EFTA–Palestinian Authority	1999	FTA
EFTA–Tunisia	2005	FTA
Egypt–Turkey	2007	FTA
Turkey–Jordan	2011	FTA

Table 8 (cont.)

Agreement	Year	Type
Turkey–Morocco	2006	FTA
Turkey–Palestinian Authority	2005	FTA
Turkey–Syria	2007	FTA
Turkey–Tunisia	2005	FTA

Source: Authors' own elaboration using the Deep Trade Agreements database
Note: CU refers to Customs Union, FTA to Free Trade Agreement, and EIA to Economic Integration Agreement.

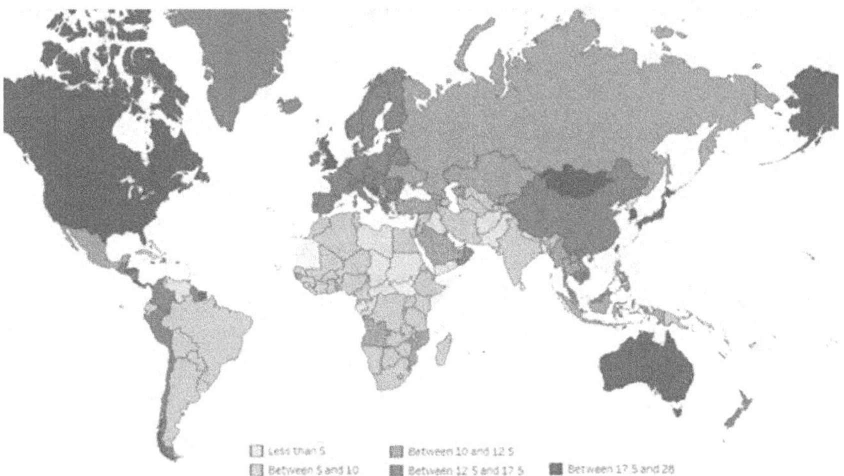

Figure 13 Average number of legally enforceable policy areas – 2021
Source: Deep Trade Agreements dataset.

low in the MENA region. Deeper agreements are clearly needed to increase trade in goods and services (Guillin et al., 2023).

Third, one can suspect that the "Spaghetti Bowl" argument holds. This concept refers to burden imposed by the multiplicity of overlapping trade agreements, which makes trade more complicated (Bhagwati, 1995). However, this is not always the case in the MENA region as shallow agreements do not entail a high cost with such an overlap.

Finally, one of the reasons that also limit the impact of some trade agreements is the list of exceptions they have. Ghoneim (2006) shows that, indeed, in the case of GAFTA, the number of exceptions (negative list) is relatively high, with several tariff lines excluded from the liberalization process. Moreover, Abedini and Peridy (2008) distinguish between two types of these exceptions: the first is related to permanent exceptions related to religious, sanitary, environmental, or security reasons. The second one pertains to temporary exceptions that cannot exceed more than 15% of each country's imports from GAFTA members.

7.1.4 Behind the Border Barriers

Behind the border barriers are important and costly. Their cost accounts for 2–15% of the value of traded goods (OECD, 2002). Such barriers are still important in low- and middle-income countries (see Figure 14) with the MENA region requiring eleven days to deliver imports and six for exports. Such figures are higher in Latin America and the Caribbean (LAC), South Asia, and sub-Saharan Africa. Yet, based on the firms' perceptions (as it is shown in Figure 15), the MENA region is the worst as 23% of firms identify customs and trade regulations as a major constraint. This figure is almost 9% in East Asia and Pacific and 17% in LAC and South Asia.

These barriers can be more costly as they are not notified at the World Trade Organization (like SPS or TBT), can affect the whole production process, and are considered a deadweight loss (no tariff revenue for instance). In addition, Hendy and Zaki (2021) show that, at the firm level, these barriers (measured by the time to trade) can be perceived as a fixed and a variable cost that affects both the extensive and the intensive margins of exports. At the product level, perishable and seasonal products are found to be more sensitive to time to trade than other products. Fontagné et al. (2020) show that advance ruling, appeal procedures, and the automation of border formalities favor large exporters, compared to small ones.

Thus, the elimination of these barriers is likely to have a highly positive impact on both international trade and welfare. This is why the WTO launched

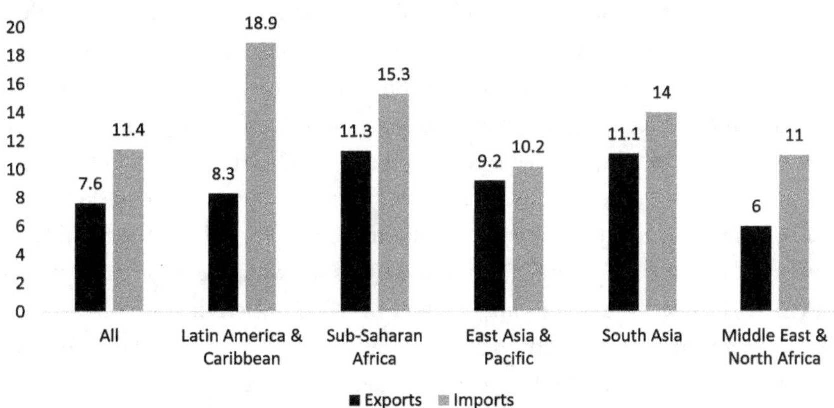

Figure 14 Days to clear direct exports and imports through customs

Source: Authors' own elaboration using the World Bank Enterprise Survey.

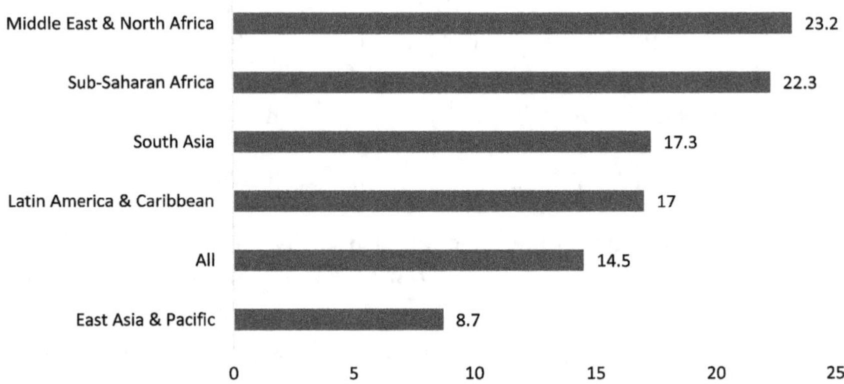

Figure 15 Percent of firms identifying customs and trade regulations
as a major constraint

Source: Authors' own elaboration using the World Bank Enterprise Survey.

the "Trade Facilitation Initiative" that led to the Trade Facilitation Agreement. The latter contains provisions for accelerating custom clearance and the delivery of goods in transit, the automation of the customs and the removal of unnecessary procedures. While WTO members ratified this agreement, non-WTO members (Algeria, Lebanon, and Libya) are still lagging behind. In addition, WTO members have different rates of the implementation of commitments with Egypt around 36% of the commitments are implemented, Morocco 90%, and Saudi Arabia 100%.

7.2 Domestic Factors

7.2.1 Institutions

Institutions can be defined as the rules of the game in a society (North, 1990). Indeed, while high-quality institutions reduce transaction costs, inefficient institutions impede trade through corruption, inadequate information, imperfect contract enforcement, higher transaction cost, and more uncertainty. Costinot (2005) and Acemoglu, Antràs and Helpman (2007), and Levchenko (2007) show, theoretically, that institutional differences can be considered as a source of comparative advantage. Thus, developing countries might not be able to generate the expected gains from trade. This is why the empirical results provide evidence of "institutional content of trade" where institutional differences are an important determinant of trade flows. In addition, the quality of institutions in levels and in differences matters for trade.

Table 9 shows that MENA countries do not have efficient institutions (both political and economic). The democracy Polity IV index ranges from 0 to 10,

Table 9 Averages of institutional variables for MENA countries (1995–2019)

Country	Democracy – Polity Index	Control of corruption	Government effectiveness	Rule of law
Algeria	3.67	−0.66	−0.66	−0.88
Bahrain	1.40	0.28	0.50	0.42
Djibouti	4.14	−0.65	−0.90	−0.86
Iran	2.35	−0.60	−0.49	−0.82
Iraq	2.46	−1.39	−1.55	−1.58
Israel	8.38	1.00	1.19	1.01
Jordan	3.67	0.14	0.09	0.31
Kuwait	2.76	0.30	0.02	0.45
Lebanon	4.70	−0.77	−0.32	−0.54
Libya	1.58	−1.17	−1.25	−1.22
Malta	9.98	0.78	1.04	1.32
Morocco	3.10	−0.22	−0.12	−0.07
Oman	1.64	0.47	0.33	0.48
Qatar	1.09	0.76	0.65	0.59
Saudi Arabia	0.12	−0.03	−0.08	0.08
Syria	0.59	−1.10	−1.09	−0.95
United Arab Emirates	1.54	0.83	1.00	0.60
Tunisia	4.40	−0.13	0.26	−0.07
Egypt	2.48	−0.59	−0.47	−0.23
Yemen	3.27	−1.13	−1.13	−1.34

Source: Authors' own elaboration using data from Freedom house Polity IV, and World Governance Indicators.

Notes: World Governance Indicators range between −2.5 (worst) and 2.5 (best). Polity index ranges between 0 (autocratic) and 10 (democratic).

where 0 is least democratic and 10 most democratic. While Malta and Israel have the highest democracy score, Saudi Arabia and Syria have the lowest one. As per economic institutions such as control of corruption, government effectiveness, and rule of law (the score ranges between −2.5 and 2.5, with higher scores corresponding to better outcomes). Among the Arab countries, the United Arab Emirates and Qatar perform better than other countries especially Libya, Yemen, and Syria. However, several countries that have low levels of political freedom as reflected by the Polity IV index have higher levels of economic freedom (measured by the index of economic freedom of the Heritage Foundation), especially GCC countries. This is why the correlation between these two variables is positive but weak and statistically insignificant (see Figure 16). For the MENA region, Karam and Zaki (2019) show that the

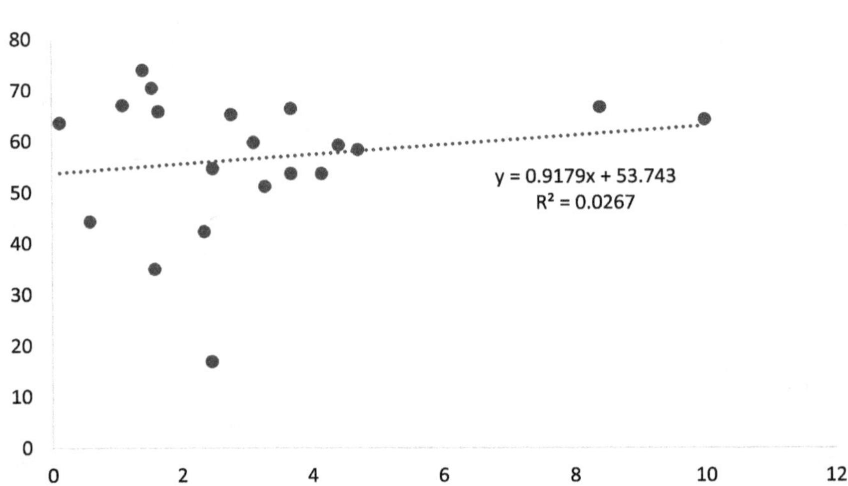

Figure 16 Correlation between economic and political freedoms

Source: Authors' own elaboration using data from Heritage Foundation and Polity IV.
Notes: Economic freedom is measured by the index of economic freedom that ranges between 0 (repressed) and 100 (free). Political freedom is measured by the Polity IV index that ranges between −10 (autocratic) and 10 (democratic).

institutional gap decreases trade and explains the high level of zero trade flows of MENA countries. Moreover, Ezzat and Zaki (2022) examine the impact of the quality of institutions on trade agreements and on exports and show that larger the difference in the quality of institutions, among MENA countries and their trade partners, the less likely they sign a trade agreement (deep compared to a shallower one), which limits the effect on exports. In addition, the more the agreement is enforced, the greater the positive effect on trade flows. This result holds for the enforcement of the provisions related to the World Trade Organization (called WTO+ and including trade liberalization of the agriculture or the industrial sector, nontariff measures, or services) and those not related to it (called WTOX and including institutions, social aspects, and regional cooperation). Therefore, the quality of institutions is indispensable for successful trade integration and compliance and enforcement of agreements.

7.2.2 Lack of Industrial Policies

Juhász et al. (2023) define industrial policies as "those government policies that explicitly target the transformation of the structure of economic activity in pursuit of some public goal" (p. 4). They argue that these policies aim at rectifying market failures to generate positive externalities, correcting coordination failures, or providing specific public inputs for some economic activities. However, such policies can suffer from two main drawbacks information gaps that can make it difficult for governments to select specific industries and the political capture where vested interests and lobbies can affect the government choice.

While most of the MENA countries lack a clear industrial policy that sets specific targets and streamlines trade policy within the industrial policy, most of the trade negotiations were primarily focusing on tariff removal and not coordinating with industrial strategies. This led to a weakly competitive industrial sector that is not able to compete with emerging economies, especially Asian and Eastern European countries. Figure 17 shows the competitive industrial performance index that benchmarks the ability of countries to produce, and export manufactured goods in a competitive way. Most of the diversified economies in the MENA region (Egypt, Tunisia, Jordan, and Morocco) have low CIP index, which shows to what extent these countries are weakly competitive, and thus their exports cannot compete worldwide. Therefore, they need deep reforms (but to a lesser extent in Morocco) to improve the competitiveness of the industrial sector.

This uncompetitive industrial sector was associated to a weak structural transformation in several diversified economies of the MENA region. Structural transformation can be defined as the case where the economy shifts its production toward higher value-added and higher productivity activities, where factors of production move from agriculture to industry then services. Marouani and Mouelhi (2016) show that, in Tunisia, despite

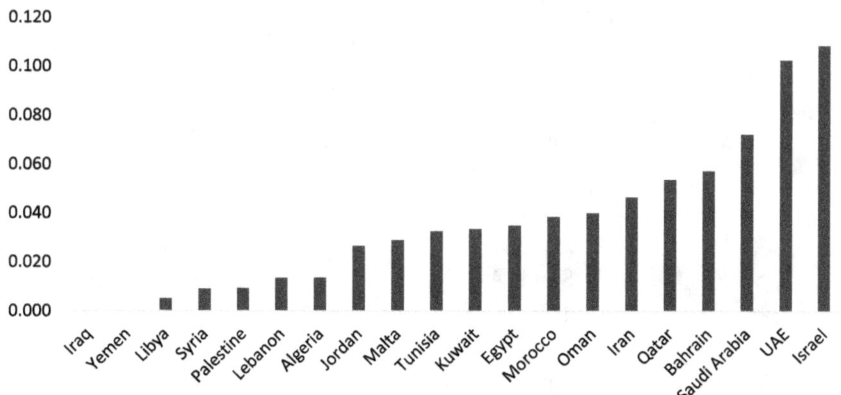

Figure 17 Competitive industrial performance index (2020)

Source: UNIDO online dataset.

Note: The CIP index is composed of eight indicators assessing industrial performance based on an economy's ability to competitively produce and export manufactured goods. Each indicator is weighted on a scale of 0 to 1. The higher the index, the more the competitive the economy.

an increase in productivity, the contribution of structural change remained very limited. In the same vein, Ben Ayed Mouelhi and Ghazali (2021) show that, for Egypt, Tunisia, and Morocco, some progress has been achieved in structural transformation between the 1970s and early 1990s. Yet, this process has stagnated and remained unfinished, leading to a deindustrialization, which further affected their structural transformation.

7.2.3 War and Conflicts

The final reason behind the poor trade performance is the prevalence of wars and conflicts in the MENA region. The latter has been suffering from different types of conflicts (armed, civil, non-state, and conflicts). Using the Armed Conflict Location and Event Data (ACLED) dataset, Table 10 shows that several MENA countries have an extreme exposure to conflicts with worsening conditions over time such as Palestine and Sudan. Moreover, Syria and Yemen have an extreme exposure as well but did not deteriorate in recent years. While Israel and Iraq have a high exposure to conflicts, Lebanon is classified as turbulent. The other countries have either a low exposure (such as Gulf countries) or have improved over

Table 10 Conflicts in the MENA region between 2019 and 2023

	Consistent	Worsening	Improving
Extreme	Syria	Palestine	–
	Yemen	Sudan	–
High	–	Israel	Iraq
	–	–	–
Turbulent	Lebanon	Iran	–
	–	–	–
	Morocco	–	Libya
	Algeria	–	Egypt
	Saudi Arabia	–	–
	Tunisia	–	–
	Jordan	–	–
Low/Inactive	Djibouti	–	–
	Malta	–	–
	Oman	–	–
	Kuwait	–	–
	Qatar	–	–
	UAE	–	–

Source: ACLED's dataset.

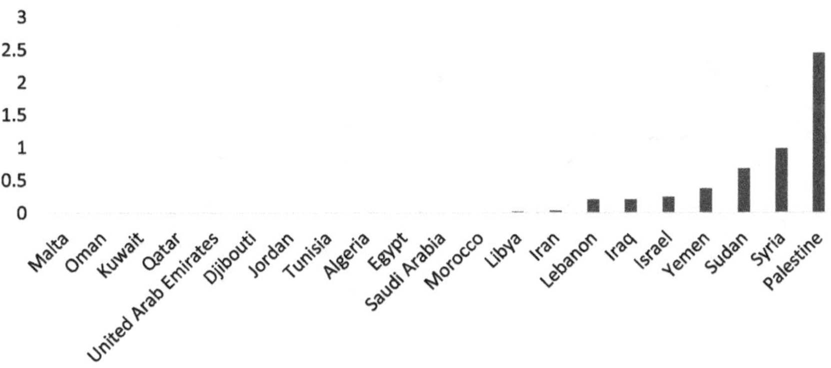

Figure 18 ACLED conflict index (2023)

Source: Authors' own elaboration using Armed Conflict Location and Event Data (ACLED).

time (such as Egypt and Libya). These facts are also confirmed by Figure 18 that shows the conflict exposure index for MENA countries.

Obviously, such conflicts can affect trade through different channels (Glick and Taylor, 2008, Martin et al., 2008 and Heilmann, 2016), especially the destruction of infrastructures, the reduction in human capital because of casualties, the deterioration of institutional quality, the imposition of partial or total trade embargoes and the increase in the costs of engaging in international trade and the opportunity cost of military spending. For the MENA region, Karam and Zaki (2016) show that wars have a significantly negative impact on exports and imports, with civil conflicts having the highest effect. In addition, they show that a conflict is equivalent to a tariff of 5% of the value of trade.

8 Trade, Business Cycles, and Growth in the MENA Region

The MENA region's performance is highly correlated with the world developments, like other emerging economies. Indeed, because we have had periods of growth and periods of recession, the objective of this section is to examine the link between trade, growth, and business cycles. Figure 19 shows that MENA growth follows closely the world GDP growth with external shocks (such as the financial crisis in 2008, the pandemic in 2020 or the war in Ukraine in 2022) or internal ones (with the Arab spring in 2011). These facts are confirmed by Figure 20. It shows that the correlation between world GDP growth and exports on the one hand and MENA growth and exports, on the other hand, is relatively high (between 60% and 70% and statistically significant).

Four main channels can explain such as high correlation. First, the MENA region receives a lot of foreign direct investment (FDI) in the oil sector. In periods

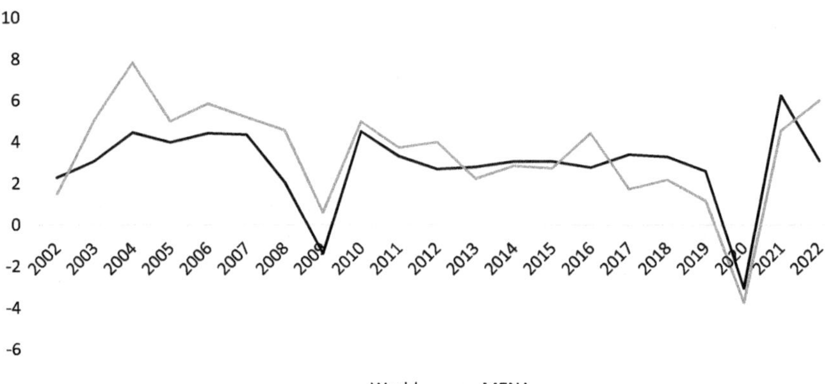

Figure 19 World business cycles and MENA

Source: Author's own elaboration using the World Development Indicators Online database.

Note: This figure shows the evolution of GDP growth at the world and the MENA level.

of recessions, such FDI inflow decreases which reduces growth and thus production and exports in MENA countries. Second, given that MENA partners are large economies (the US and EU), once the latter experience any shock that affects their demand, they import less, which leads to lower exports from the MENA region. Third, the MENA (especially oil-importing countries) are large recipients of remittances. Thus, whenever there is a world recession, less remittances are channels to MENA countries, which affects the demand and thus growth. Finally, being the largest exporter of oil, the MENA region is largely affected by the developments of oil world prices. This is confirmed by Figure 21 that plots the correlation between the change in oil prices and the change in MENA exports.

Clearly, and being relatively integrated in the global economy, trade changes affect growth in the MENA region. The nexus between trade and growth has been thoroughly studied in the literature (Krueger, 1990; Dollar and Kraay, 2003; Lopez, 2005; and Frankel and Romer, 2017). For the MENA region, Karam and Zaki (2015) shows that trade contributes significantly to growth. Contribution to growth is computed by multiplying the share of trade in goods (in services) to GDP by its growth rate for a particular year (see Figure 22). Obviously, in the MENA region, trade in goods has substantially contributed to the GDP growth more than trade in services. The latter are still suffering from different regulations and rules that make them relatively protected and thus contribute less to growth. Figure 23 shows that the MENA region has indeed one of the highest service trade restrictiveness index, compared to other countries and a lot of countries have low services commitments at the WTO (Karam and Zaki, 2013). In addition, since the 2000s, regional trade agreements have included provisions related to services.

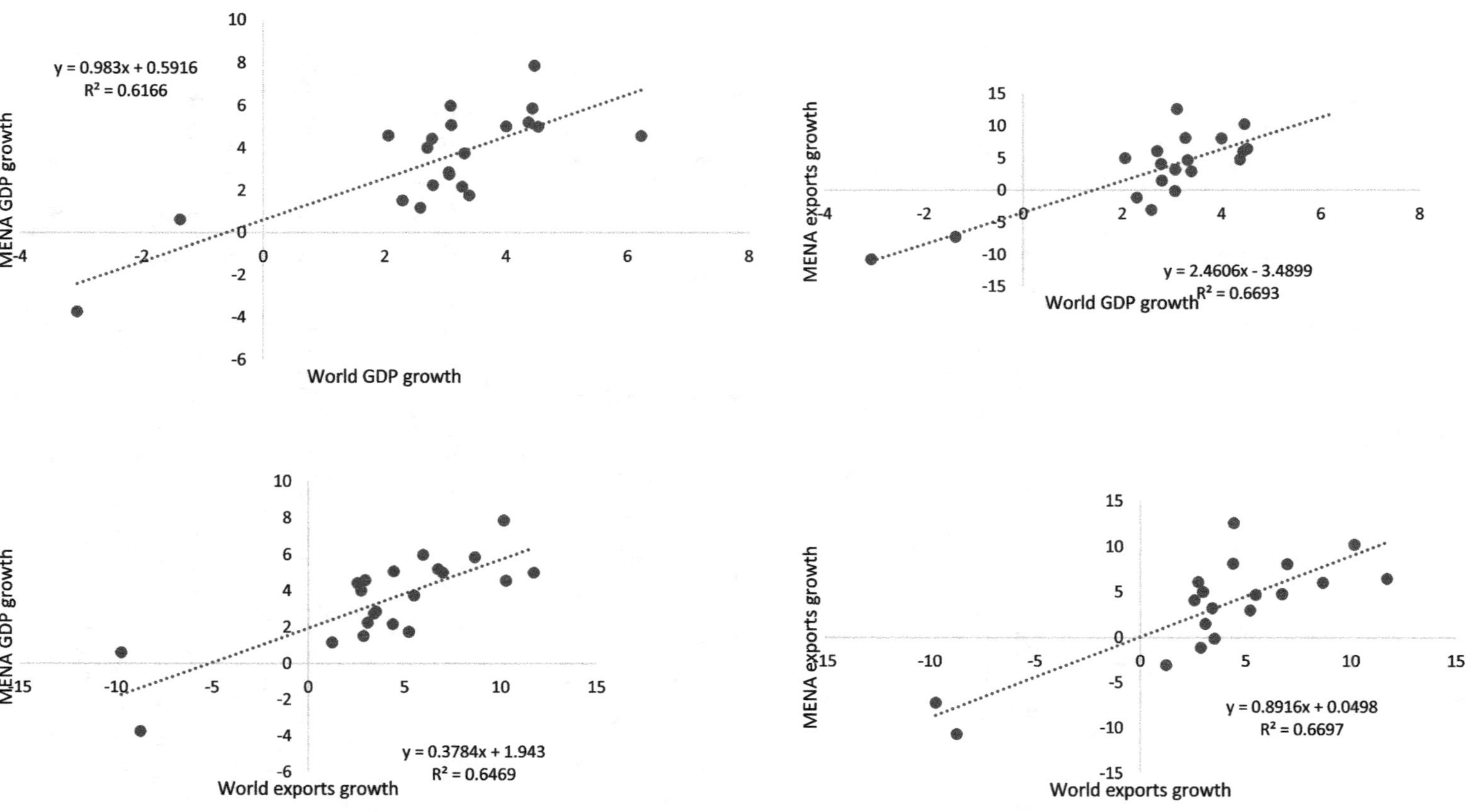

Figure 20 Correlations between the MENA region and the world

Source: Author's own elaboration using the World Development Indicators Online database.

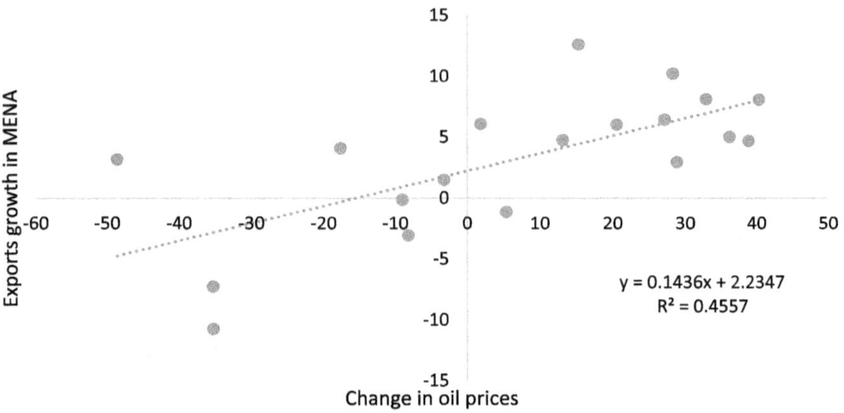

Figure 21 Change in oil prices and exports growth in the MENA region

Source: Authors' own elaboration using the World Development Indicators Online database and OPEC Crude Oil dataset.

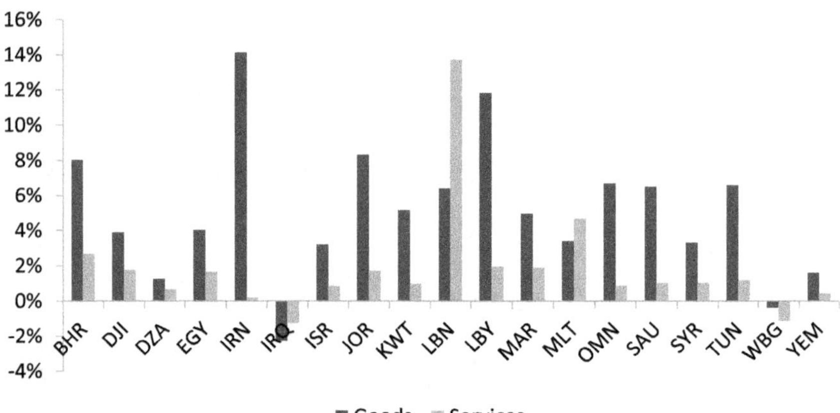

Figure 22 Contribution of trade in goods and trade in services to growth (average by country)

Source: Karam and Zaki (2015).

Guillin et al. (2023) show that deep trade agreements boost the quantity of service exports and lead to their diversification. However, for the MENA regions, most of the agreements are rather shallow and deal with tariff liberalization without addressing harmonization of rules and regulations or nontariff measures (Kheir El Din and Ghoneim (2005) and Aboushady et al. (2021)). Furthermore, most of the agreements include a limited number of legally enforceable provisions, which reduces their effects on trade in services.

Moreover, while trade in goods contributed more to economic growth, it still not fully utilized as the technology transfer related to trade is still limited for

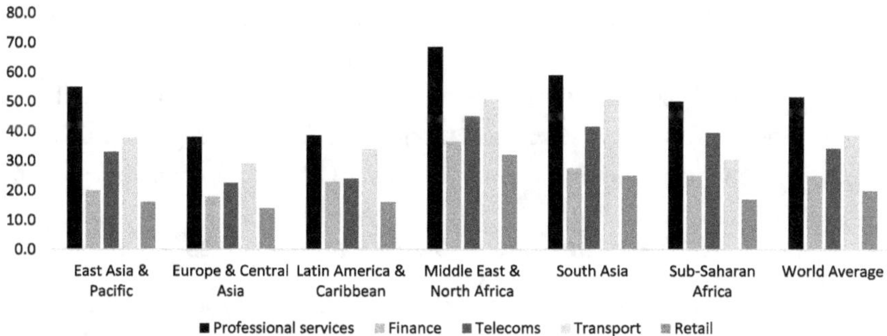

Figure 23 Service trade restrictiveness index – by region and sector
Source: OECD.

several reasons. First, as argued by Costantini and Liberati (2014), technology transfer needs efficient institutions (especially antitrust regulation and competition agencies and intellectual property rights). Having deficient institutions, most of the MENA countries (with the exception of Morocco) were not able to diffuse global technologies with both factor and product markets. Second, in addition to consumption goods, a large share of MENA imports includes intermediate inputs. Yet, with a relatively weak industrial base, these countries were not able to upgrade and diversify their production structure. Finally, the spillover effect from FDI to technology depends on the characteristics of incoming FDI (Sinani and Meyer, 2004). More specifically, given that most of the FDI inflow was either in the real estate or oil sectors (and refineries), there was little room to increase technology transfer in sectors that have limited value-added and that have weak backward and forward linkages with the rest of the economy. Finally, given that services matter for technology transfer, most of the regional agreements of the MENA region do not have legally enforceable provisions related to services (Guillin et al., 2023).

This lack of technology transfer is line with the findings of World Bank (2024) that argues that, to avoid the middle-income trap, developing countries need to adopt the 3i strategy: investment, infusion, innovation. In fact, to transition from the low-income to lower-middle income countries category, policy-makers need to move from a 1i strategy that accelerates investment to a 2i strategy that focuses on investment and infusion. The latter refers to the case where investment strategies help infuse modern technologies from abroad into the domestic economy. After this transition, the second transition to the upper-middle income category needs the third i pertaining to innovation. While most of MENA countries managed to invest a lot, only a few managed to infuse the imported technology (Morocco) and to innovate (Israel).

In a nutshell, while the MENA region is moderately integrated in the world economy, its economic growth is correlated to the evolution of oil prices, world exports, and world economic growth. In addition, with a more pronounced liberalization of goods relative to services that remained relatively regulated and protected, the former contributed more than the latter to MENA's economic growth.

9 Trade and Development Outcomes

After examining the different characteristics of trade flows and policies in the MENA region, it is important to examine how the latter affected different development outcomes. Indeed, the literature has shown that trade policy can affect gender and labor market, among other outcomes.

9.1 Labor Market

The nexus between trade and labor market has been widely studied in the literature. Several theories could be evoked in this regard (Zaki, 2014). First, the Heckscher-Ohlin-Samuelson (1933 and 1941) model was one of the first attempts. According to the Stolper-Samuelson effect, an increase in the relative price of a good (where the country has a comparative advantage) will lead to a more than proportional increase in the real returns of the factor which is intensively used in the production of that good, and conversely, to a fall in the real returns of the other factor if production factors are mobile between sectors. Yet, inter-sectoral mobility of the factors of production is relatively low in the short run. This is why the sector specific model (Viner, 1953) assumes that one factor of production is specific to a particular industry. A movement toward free trade increases the price of the exportable goods and reduces that of importable ones. Hence, the return of the factors used in the exporting sectors will increase while factors used in the importing sectors will witness a decline of their revenues. Therefore, both labor demand and wages can be affected by the performance of exports and imports. Similar observations can be observed for the demand for formal vs. informal and skilled vs. unskilled labor. We focus in this part on three outcomes that matter from a development perspective, which are informal employment, wage inequality, and the composition of labor.

Informal employment is a key issue in the MENA region given that several workers do not have either a contract nor a social insurance scheme (Adair et al., 2024). While this sector represents a buffer during crises, its workers are highly vulnerable. When it comes to trade policy, Selwaness and Zaki (2015) and Ben Salem and Zaki (2019) show that, in Egypt, trade liberalization can improve labor market outcomes by reducing informal employment. This is due to the fact that, with lower tariffs, only the most productive firms can face this fiercer competition, leading to a higher demand for skilled workers that are likely to be formal. Similar findings have been confirmed by Karam and Zaki (2024) for Egypt, Jordan, Morocco, Tunisia, and Sudan. They argue that this effect is more pronounced post COVID pandemic. In addition, this formalization probability is higher for blue collars and men that are employed more intensively in sectors where MENA countries have a comparative advantage.

Second, ***wage inequality*** can be affected by trade openness. This inequality can be observed at the several levels, especially the industry wage premia, between skilled and unskilled workers, and between females and males. On the skill premium, several studies show that, with trade liberalization, sector-biased technical change can significantly increase skilled labor's relative wages (Feenstra and Hanson, 2001 and Attanasio et al., 2004). At the gender level, among the very first studies, Becker (1971) showed that, theoretically, free trade implies a more competitive environment and, consequently, a less discriminating economy. However, the empirical literature shows that this effect depends on the intensity of women in different sectors, different formal and informal institutions, and the country's comparative advantage. For the MENA region, Aboushady et al. (2021) show that for Egypt, Jordan, and Tunisia, wage disparities are affected by tariffs and nontariff measures. This is confirmed by Figure 24 that shows that wages are in general higher for more open sectors. Yet, while females are more affected by nontariff measures than their male counterparts, production workers are less affected by both nontariff measures and by services restrictions than non-production workers but more affected by tariffs. This is primarily due to the abundancy of blue collars in the MENA region.

Third, for the ***composition of labor***, Aboushady and Zaki (2021), using the World Bank Enterprise Survey for MENA countries, show that exporting firms are

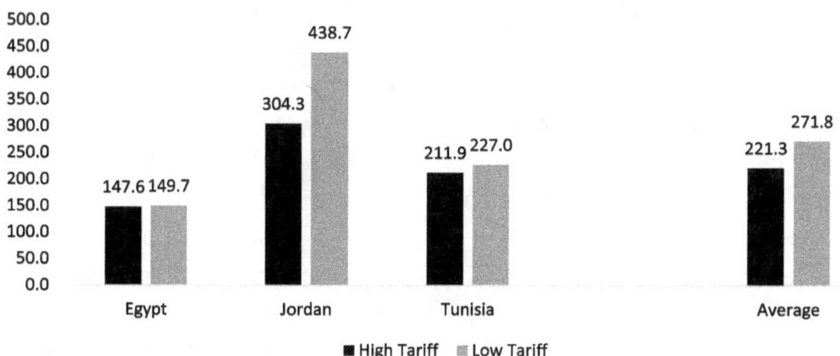

Figure 24 Wages and tariffs

Source: Aboushady et al. (2021) using ILMPS.

Note: (i) Figures represent real monthly wage in constant USD (2010). (ii) High tariff means a sector with a tariff greater than the median one.

more likely to innovate, which, in turn, increases the demand for skilled production workers. This is primarily due to the fact that most of the sectors where the MENA countries have a comparative advantage are intensive in blue collars (such textiles, ready-made garments, chemicals, and processed food). This result is in line with the Skilled Bias Technological Change (Feenstra and Hanson, 2001), according to which the trade liberalization is associated to a fiercer competition that requires a stronger technological progress. This will shift demand away from low-skilled activities and raise the relative demand and wages of the better-skilled (Goldberg and Pavcnik, 2004 for Colombia for instance).

9.2 Gender

The second development outcome we are interested in is gender. The literature on gender and labor market in the MENA region is rather abundant and is characterized by the following (Assaad, 2014 and Assaad and Kraftf, 2014). First, Assaad et al. (2020) argue that this region has a paradox as, despite rising female educational attainment, female labor force participation rates remain low and stagnant. This is primarily due to the contraction in public sector employment opportunities and limited job creation in the private sector. Second, this low participation can also be attributed to individual characteristics. Hayo and Caris (2013) show that identity matters. Indeed, while Muslim women do not participate in the labor market less than non-Muslim women, those with strong traditional identities tend to participate less. Finally, marriage also plays a role as shown by Assaad et al. (2022). The authors show marriage, being *a central stage in the transition to adulthood*, reduces women's probability of market work by 47% in Jordan, 30% in Tunisia, and 16% in Egypt.

Against this background, trade affects, and is affected by, gender. On the one hand, trade can exert different effects on gender through different channels. First, from a theoretical perspective, free trade is associated with a more competitive environment and, as a result, a less discriminating economy, as demonstrated by Becker (1971). Second, freer trade can lead to the expansion of exporting sectors, and if the latter are women-intensive (such as textiles and ready-made garments), the demand for women increases. Third, another strand of literature shows that trade liberalization leads to a decline in the gender wage gap. For instance, Aguayo-Tellez et al. (2014) argue that, in Mexico, women's wage bill share grew as employment increased. In Egypt, Zaki (2014) shows that red tape barriers have a higher impact than traditional tariffs on wage disparity with female and blue-collar workers being more affected. Fourth, trade policy can affect women empowerment through trade agreements. In a more recent work, Karam and Zaki (2024) show that the inclusion of gender-related provisions in trade agreements

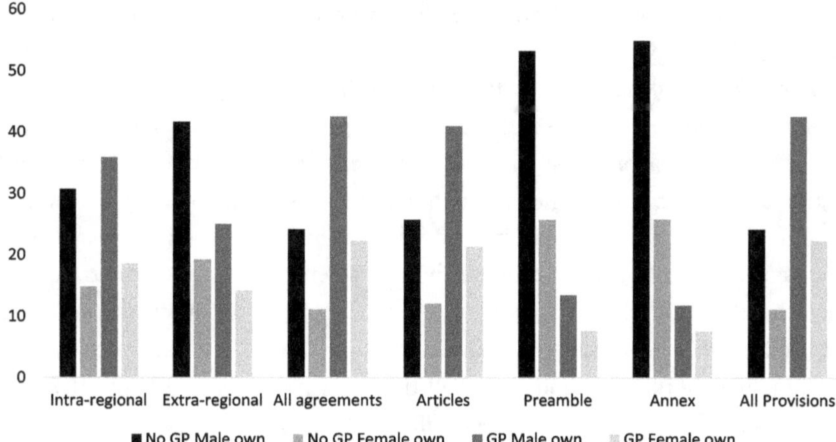

Figure 25 Female vs. male owned firms and RTAs with vs. without gender provisions

Source: Authors' own elaboration based on Karam and Zaki (2024).

increases the likelihood of women ownership. Yet, this effect depends on the location of the provisions. Indeed, if the provisions are in the core of the agreement (not the preamble or the annex), the impact is stronger as the provisions are more enforceable. Figure 25 shows that the share of female ownership increases from 11% of firms to 22% when the agreements (intra- or extra-regional agreements) include a gender-related provision.

In terms of the impact of gender on trade, Karam and Zaki (2021) show that, for the MENA region, show that female labor participation has a positive a significant impact on both the probability of export and export volume. In addition, female ownership exerts a positive effect on the probability of large firms to export, shedding light on the importance of female empowerment in international trade. However, it is important to note that the effect of some investment barriers on exports is more pronounced for a female-owned/managed firm, compared to a male-owned/managed one.

10 Summary and Conclusions

The objective of this Element is to present the main characteristics of international trade in the Middle East and North Africa (MENA) region by analyzing whether its trade policy managed to build or break bridges among MENA countries and with the rest of the world. Its objective is threefold. First, it provides a historical background and an overview of trade theories from the MENA region perspective. Second, it analyzes the main trends and features of trade flows and trade policies. Third, it shows how trade policies had different development outcomes related to gender, informal employment and the composition of labor demand.

The Middle East and North Africa (MENA) region plays an important role in the global economy. This is due to its strategic location, its abundant natural resources, and historical significance as a crossroads of trade. Despite the region's pivotal role in the global economy, MENA's economic growth is highly volatile due to oil price volatility and political instability. This region is also composed of heterogeneous countries with different trade structures and various growth paths. Oil-exporting countries, particularly in the Gulf Cooperation Council (GCC), have engaged in diversification strategies to mitigate dependency on oil exports. Oil-importing countries in the region have focused on being more competitive in sectors like agriculture, tourism, and manufacturing.

MENA region experienced a significant liberalization over time but remained weakly integrated in the global economy. Trade liberalization measures, such as the reduction of tariff and nontariff barriers, and trade facilitation initiatives, have been implemented to promote trade openness. Moreover, MENA countries have joined different bilateral and regional trade agreements to enhance trade flows among neighboring countries. Examples include the Greater Arab Free Trade Area (GAFTA) aiming at promoting trade openness among Arab countries, and the Euro-Mediterranean Trade Agreement between the European Union and multiple Mediterranean countries.

The objective of this Element is to examine to what extent MENA's efforts are effective in building or breaking bridges at the regional and global levels. In other words, it tries to investigate to what extent the region is able to connect and integrate both regionally and globally, or whether could some countries be, unintentionally or deliberately, taking actions that break those bridges and hinder the desired regional global integration. Hence, this Element tells the story of trade in the MENA region, exploring historical backgrounds, the applicability of international trade theories, trade patterns and policies, as well as the relation between trade and economic growth.

Based on our analysis of trade in the MENA region, several key conclusions emerge. First, the MENA region experienced liberalization without real integration. Indeed, shallow trade agreements and persistent trade barriers, especially nontariff measures, high tariffs, and costly administrative barriers, in addition to weak institutions and lack of industrial competitiveness, explain the relatively poor performance of trade flows in most of the diversified MENA economies. Second, the MENA region is highly affected by the world business cycles given that the region is highly dependent on oil revenues. Therefore, in order to increase the region resilience, a stronger diversification should take place at the partners and the products levels. Moreover, trade policy should not be limited to the reduction of tariff barriers, but has to be broadened to other nontariff impediments, service regulations, and development-related issues, and should be accompanied by other reforms to improve the business environment and the quality of institutions and infrastructure.

11 Policy Implications

First, it is important to recall that the MENA region is not a homogeneous region as it includes oil-exporting countries, diversified ones, and conflict-affected ones. This calls for tailored policies for each group to improve their integration in the world economy. Second, the historical ties of the MENA region are equally important as they help explain why many countries trade a lot with its former colonizing countries. In addition, with the ISI that were implemented, most of these countries failed to have more effective export promotion policies. Third, both the macroeconomic and the microeconomic analyses show to what extent the MENA region is not sufficiently diversified as most of exporting firms are oil exporters, which affects the countries' integration into GVCs.

Against this background, one can claim that the MENA region experienced liberalization without real integration. In fact, trade policies (especially non-tariff measures, high tariffs, and costly administrative barriers and shallow trade agreements) and domestic characteristics (weak institutions and lack of indus-trial competitiveness) explain the relatively poor performance of trade flows in most of the diversified MENA economies. In addition, the MENA region is highly affected by the world business cycles (especially through oil prices) given that this region is the largest exporter of oil. Finally, development outcomes still need to be streamlined within trade policies.

From a policy perspective, three important implications emanate from this analysis. First, in order to increase the MENA region resilience, a stronger diversification must take place at the partners and the products level. This will need to attract more FDI in the manufacturing sector to increase backward and forward linkages with other sectors, improve the exports of industrial products, and boost the countries' integration into GVCs.

Second, trade policy must be accompanied by other policies and reforms to be effective. For the business environment, streamlining procedures and redu-cing the red tape cost associated to starting a business are essential for a more dynamic private sector. Moreover, competition policies need to be more enforced and more transparent. This will help strengthen the role of the private sector as the main driver of growth and jobs and the role of the state as a catalyst for private sector development. This will need a transparent state ownership policy and governance framework and legal reforms to strengthen the framework for public enterprises.

Third, several reforms are needed to the quality of institutions (that need to become more investor friendly), infrastructure, and the conception and the implementation of clearer industrial strategies (that are more connected to exports strategies). A better infrastructure will reduce the transport and behind-the-border costs, which will facilitate trade. This needs to be coupled with more automation of customs to reduce corruption and increase the delivery of imported and exported products, which will positively affect integration intro GVC (Guedidi et al., 2025).

Fourth, supply-related factors that consider the country's competitiveness must be combined with demand-related factors (measured by global import growth rates). Thus, products with a high comparative advantage and high global demand should become the top priority. Those that have a high comparative advantage and a low global demand should be perceived as a tool to increase exports in the short term. In contrast, products with a low comparative advantage and high global demand shall need the government support to increase their comparative advantage.

Finally, a paradigm shift is needed regarding the perception of trade policy. To move forward, the latter must not be limited to tariff removal or reduction but must be broadened to other nontariff impediments, service regulations, and development-related issues. The latter means that trade policy must be more inclusive for vulnerable categories such as women, informal workers, and unskilled ones.

Appendix

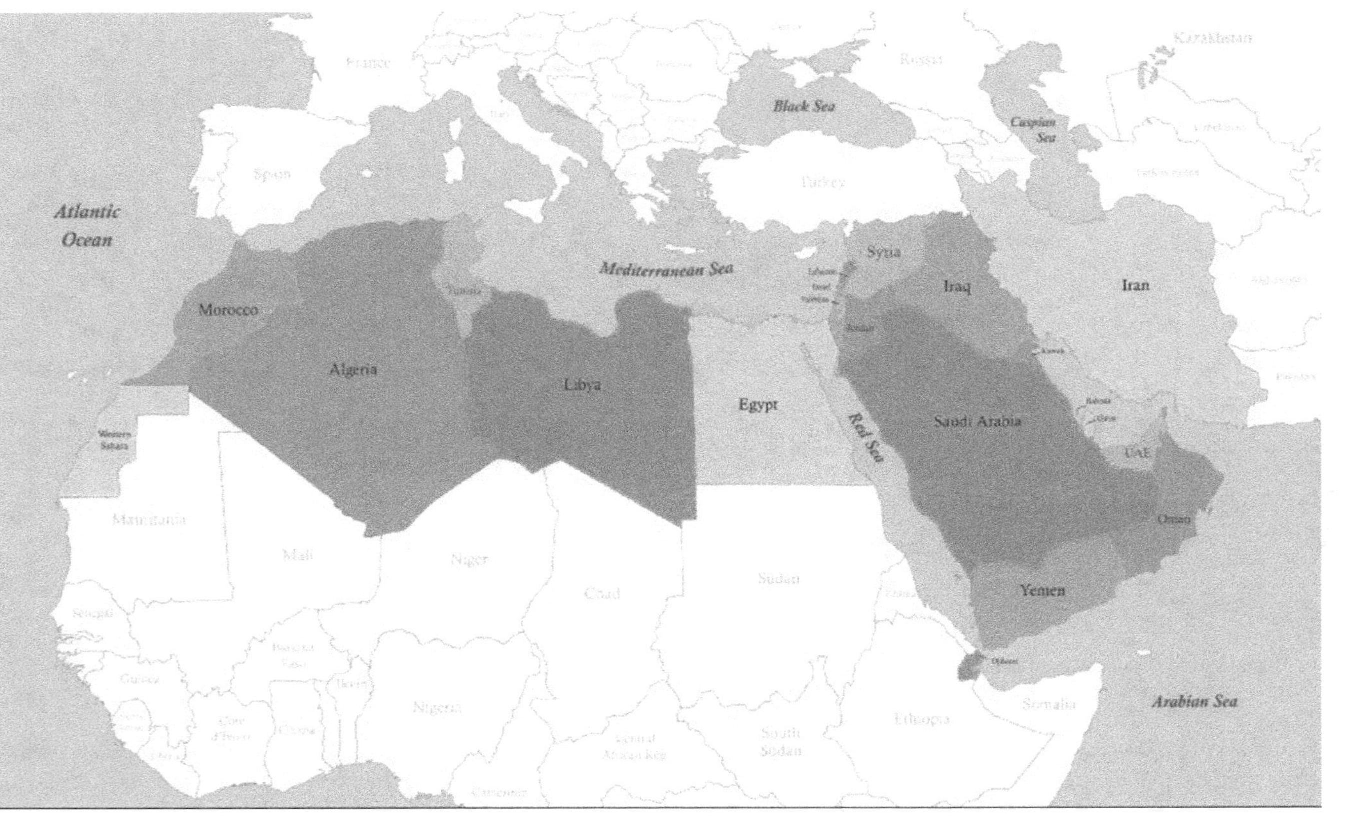

Figure A.1 Map of the MENA region

Source: https://www.vectorstock.com/royalty-free-vector/mena-region-political-map-vector-46399256

Table **A.1** Periods for import substitution strategies (ISI) and export-oriented industrialization (EOI), by country

Country	Period for ISI	Period for EOI
Algeria	1960s–1980s	1990s
Bahrain	1980s–1990s	2000s
Djibouti	1970s–1990s	2000s
Egypt	1960s–1980s	1980s–1990s
Iran	1960s–1970s	1980s–1990s
Iraq	1960s–1980s	Limited (pre–1990s)
Israel	1950s–1970s	1980s–1990s
Jordan	1970s–1990s	1990s–2000s
Kuwait	1960s–1980s	1990s
Lebanon	1970s–1990s	1990s–2000s
Libya	1960s–1980s	1990s
Malta	1970s–1990s	2000s
Morocco	1960s–1980s	1990s
Oman	1970s–1990s	2000s
West Bank and Gaza	1970s–1990s	2000s
Qatar	1970s–1990s	2000s

Source: Constructed by the authors from various sources.

Table A.2 Trade in services – by sector and country – 2021 (%)

	Maintenance and repair services n.i.e.	Transport	Travel	Insurance and pension services	Financial services	Telecommunications, computer, and information services	Other business services	Government goods and services n.i.e.	Other	Total
MENA oil exporters										
GCC countries										
Bahrain	10.7	0.0	0.0	2.2	0.0	58.6	0.0	9.9	18.7	100.0
Kuwait	0.1	0.0	10.5	12.5	5.4	18.2	4.4	46.1	2.8	100.0
Oman	22.9	0.0	0.0	35.9	20.9	3.3	1.0	13.9	2.1	100.0
Qatar	0.0	61.6	23.2	5.6	0.0	4.8	0.0	3.6	1.1	100.0
Saudi Arabia	2.0	0.0	5.8	25.9	37.1	1.1	13.9	14.2	0.0	100.0
UAE	5.6	3.3	1.0	24.3	33.8	17.5	1.6	7.3	5.6	100.0
Non-GCC countries										
Algeria	58.9	0.2	1.9	17.2	2.2	2.7	7.7	2.7	6.6	100.0
Iran	4.3	0.0	2.8	23.9	59.2	0.5	1.1	1.5	6.6	100.0
Iraq	25.0	0.1	7.1	8.6	37.9	0.1	0.1	3.7	17.4	100.0
Libya	0.0	0.0	11.1	28.6	12.5	30.8	0.0	17.0	0.0	100.0
Yemen	0.8	0.0	36.6	26.8	0.0	0.0	0.0	35.9	0.0	100.0

MENA oil importers

Djibouti	0.0	0.0	31.5	56.7	3.8	0.0		0.0	8.0	0.0	100.0
Egypt	4.3	0.4	4.6	39.0	40.6	1.8		1.0	6.4	1.8	100.0
Israel	36.1	0.8	0.1	8.5	4.7	0.1		3.3	37.0	9.6	100.0
Jordan	4.9	3.5	3.6	21.2	61.2	0.0		2.5	0.7	2.3	100.0
Lebanon	27.0	1.3	0.5	2.4	53.6	4.8		3.2	4.1	3.1	100.0
Malta	20.5	0.0	0.6	7.9	4.3	4.7		7.9	0.9	53.2	100.0
Morocco	23.5	0.6	3.7	18.7	24.9	1.1		0.4	12.7	14.5	100.0
Syria	0.5	0.7	4.0	7.2	84.4	0.2		0.9	1.9	0.1	100.0
Tunisia	3.1	0.3	4.6	29.4	35.0	2.8		2.6	10.1	12.0	100.0
Palestine	0.1	0.6	72.2	0.0	0.0	4.6		1.8	3.5	17.2	100.0

Source: Authors' own elaboration using ITC online database. All data are those of 2021 except for Bahrain (2020), Iran (2019), Libya (2020), Yemen (2020), Israel (2020), and Syria (2010).

Table A.3 Firms identifying each constraint as a major barrier

Economy Year	Djibouti 2013	Egypt 2020	Iraq 2022	Israel 2013	Jordan 2019	Lebanon 2019	Malta 2019	Morocco 2023	Saudi Arabia 2022	Tunisia 2020	WBG 2023	Yemen 2013
						Non-exporter						
Access to finance	1.2	8.9	24.5	4	2.9	29.4	6.2	2.5	13.8	39.2	19.7	4.7
Access to land	0.5	0.2	6.7	0.6	1.9	0.4	3.5	5.2	22.8	0.5	1.4	1.6
Business licensing and permits	1.1	5.8	12.1	14	2.4	0.7	0	4.2	10.6	4.3	1.5	0
Corruption	12.3	13.8	14.5	0.5	15.2	12.4	2.3	14.2	1.7	18.2	8	8.2
Courts	0.9	0.2	0.5	0	2.1	0	0.7	0.9	0	0.6	2	0.8
Crime, theft and disorder	0	0.5	0.4	0.2	1.2	0.2	0.9	2.5	0.1	0.4	1.3	8.5
Customs and trade regulations	2	4.3	5.5	2	7.2	1.5	1.6	6.6	2.2	4.8	4	0.8
Electricity	53.6	3.1	8.3	0.2	10.2	5.9	1.7	1.4	2.9	0.5	3.4	19.2
Inadequately educated workforce	6	2.1	1.3	33.9	0.2	0.5	40.7	11.1	14.8	5.5	1.7	0.8
Labor regulations	1.6	1.6	2	1.3	7.2	0.3	3.2	9.5	11	2.1	2.3	1.4
Political instability	1.2	17.4	9.9	12.5	12.3	36.8	0.8	5.2	0	11.2	34.9	51.9
Informal sector	2.7	8.7	6	3.2	3.1	7.1	13.8	18.9	10.3	8.7	6.1	1.1
Tax administration	1.2	6.6	1.8	2	2.7	0	0	9.1	1.2	0.5	2.6	0.3
Tax rates	13.4	25.4	5.8	22.1	28.5	4.4	3.7	4	4	3.1	10	0.3
Transportation	2.4	1.6	0.8	3.5	3.1	0.5	20.8	4.6	4.6	0.4	1.1	0.2

Source: World Bank Enterprise Survey.

Table A.4 Firms identifying each constraint as a major barrier

| | Exporter | | | | | | | | | | | |
	Djibouti 2013	Egypt 2020	Iraq 2022	Israel 2013	Jordan 2019	Lebanon 2019	Malta 2019	Morocco 2023	Saudi Arabia 2022	Tunisia 2020	WBG 2023	Yemen 2013
Access to finance	0	1.6	28.9	10.6	0.5	26.2	17.7	3.6	5.5	42.3	4.9	0
Access to land	3.1	0.3	1.3	1.6	0.4	0	0	3.6	3.7	0.8	0.1	0
Business licensing and permits	3.1	6.4	10.5	1.7	0.4	0	0	0	15.7	7.8	19.7	0
Corruption	10	26.9	10.8	0.3	18.6	10.8	0	19.8	8.5	5.7	4.5	5
Courts	0	0	0	0.2	0	0.4	0	1.2	0.1	0	0	0.8
Crime, theft and disorder	0	0.9	0	3.8	0	0.1	1.3	0.5	0.2	0.2	4.5	0.9
Customs and trade regulations	12	10.2	5.9	0.6	4	4.7	8.4	1.2	0.9	5.8	1.9	0
Electricity	34.3	3.6	20.6	4.4	19	1.2	9.1	0	7.9	1.1	8.7	70.1
Inadequately educated workforce	14.6	3.3	5.4	14.8	0.1	0.4	24.4	0.5	11	5.3	2.3	0
Labor regulations	3.1	8.5	2.1	7.1	3.6	0	5.7	0.7	3	6.9	10.3	0
Political instability	0	17.5	0	29.8	17.7	36.2	2.9	8	0	11.9	24.2	21.9
Informal sector	4.6	8.2	0	1.2	5.6	3.8	5	35.5	40.9	3.4	10.2	1
Tax administration	2.4	2.3	1.6	0.2	0.7	0	0	7.1	2	3	2.9	0.3
Tax rates	10.5	10.3	12.9	10.8	26.7	16.2	7.9	13	0.6	3.7	5.3	0
Transportation	2.3	0	0	13	2.8	0	17.6	5.2	0	2	0.5	0

References

Abedini, N. and Peridy, J. (2008). "The Greater Arab Free Trade Area: An Estimation of Trade Effects," *Journal of Economic Integration*, 23(4), 848–872.

Aboushady, N. and Zaki, C. (2019) "Investment Climate and Trade Margins in Egypt: Which Factors Do Matter?," *Economics Bulletin*, 39(4), 2275–2301.

Aboushady N. and Zaki, C. (2023). "Trade Policy and Food Security in Turbulent Times," in S. Capasso and G. Canitano (eds.), *Mediterranean Economies*, Il Mulino. https://www.mulino.it/isbn/9788815387783.

Aboushady, N., Kamal, Y. and Zaki, C. (2022). "Disentangling the Impact of Trade Barriers on Wages: Evidence from the MENA Region," *Middle East Development Journal*, 14(1), 43–69.

Aboushady, N. and Zaki, C. (2021). "Do Exports and Innovation Matter for the Demand of Skilled Labor?" *International Review of Applied Economics*, 35(1), 25–44.

Aboushady N. and Zaki, C. (2021). "Assessing EU-Middle East Trade Relations: Patterns, Policies and Imbalances," in D. Bouris, D. Huber, and M. Pace, (eds.), *Routledge Handbook on EU-Middle East Relations,* https://www.routledge.com/Routledge-Handbook-of-EUMiddle-East-Relations/Bouris-Huber-Pace/p/book/9780367330767?fbclid=IwAR2Fe-QbVQEMFIUj1PMcjOu27YnmJC3Ue1Vr49GN5Ne_mhCAhjGEssvkVGU.

Aboushady N. and Zaki, C. (2025) "Political connections and participation in global value chains: Evidence from MENA firms", European Journal of Political Economy (forthcoming).

Acemoglu, D., Antràs, P. and Helpman, E. (2007). "Contracts and Technology Adoption," *American Economic Review*, 97(3), 916–943.

Acharyya, R. and Ganguly, S. (2023). "Export Quality and Income Distribution," Series: Cambridge Elements in International Economics, Cambridge University Press, Online ISBN: 9781009128995, https://doi.org/10.1017/9781009128995.

Adair, P., AlAzzawi, S. and Hlasny, V. (2024). "Fostering Decent Jobs, Formalising Informal Employment and Spurring Job Mobility in MENA Countries," *Economic Notes*, 53(2), e12240.

Aghion, P. (2002). "Schumpeterian Growth Theory and the Dynamics of Income Inequality," *Econometrica*, 70(3), 855–882.

Aguayo-Tellez, E., Airola, J., Juhn, C., and Villegas-Sanchez, C. (2014). Did Trade Liberalization Help Women? The Case of Mexico in the 1990s. In *New Analyses of Worker Well-Being* (pp. 1–35). Emerald Group Publishing Limited.

Álvarez, I. C., Barbero, J., Rodríguez-Pose, A. and Zofío, J. L. (2018). "Does Institutional Quality Matter for Trade? Institutional Conditions in a Sectoral Trade Framework," *World Development*, 103, 72–87.

Amiti, M. and Konings, J. (2007). "Trade Liberalization, Intermediate Inputs, and Productivity: Evidence from Indonesia," *American Economic Review*, 97(5), 1611–1638.

Anderson, James E. (1979). "A Theoretical Foundation for the Gravity Equation," *American Economic Review*, 69, 106–116.

Anderson, James E. and Eric Van Wincoop (2003). "Gravity with Gravitas: A Solution to the Border Puzzle," *American Economic Review*, 93, 170–192.

Anderson, J. and van Wincoop, E. (2004). "Trade Costs," *Journal of Economic Literature*, XLII, 691–751.

Assaad, R., Hendy, R., Lassassi, M. and Yassin, S. (2020). "Explaining the MENA Paradox: Rising Educational Attainment, Yet Stagnant Female Labor Force Participation," *Demographic Research*, 43, 817.

Assaad, R. (2014). "Making Sense of Arab Labor Markets: The Enduring Legacy of Dualism," *IZA Journal of Labor & Development*, 3, 1–25.

Assaad, R. and Krafft, C. (2014). An Empirical Analysis of the Economics of Marriage in Egypt, Morocco, and Tunisia, Oxford Handbooks Online, https://academic.oup.com/edited-volume/34501/chapter-abstract/292736143?redirectedFrom=fulltext.

Assaad, R., Krafft, C. and Selwaness, I. (2022). "The Impact of Marriage on Women's Employment in the Middle East and North Africa," *Feminist Economics*, 28(2), 247–279.

Ayed Mouelhi, R. B. and Ghazali, M. (2021). "Structural Transformation in Egypt, Morocco and Tunisia: Patterns, Drivers and Constraints," *Economics of Transition and Institutional Change*, 29(1), 35–61.

Ayadi, R., Giovannetti, G., Marvasi, E. and Zaki, C. (2024). "Trade Networks and the Productivity of MENA Firms in Global Value Chains," *Structural Change and Economic Dynamics*, 69, 10–23.

Ayadi, R., Giovannetti, G., Marvasi, E., Vannelli, G. and Zaki, C. (2022). "Demand and Supply Exposure through Global Value Chains: Euro-Mediterranean Countries during COVID," *The World Economy*, 45(3), 637–656.

Ayed Mouelhi, R. B. and Ghazali, M. (2021). "Structural Transformation in Egypt, Morocco and Tunisia: Patterns, Drivers and Constraints," *Economics of Transition and Institutional Change*, 29(1), 35–61.

Baldwin, R. (2013). "Trade and Industrialization after Globalization's Second Unbundling: How Building and Joining a Supply Chain Are Different and Why It Matters," in *Globalization in an Age of Crisis: Multilateral Economic*

Cooperation in the Twenty-First Century. Chicago: University of Chicago Press, pp. 165–212.

Bas, M. (2012). "Input-Trade Liberalization and Firm Export Decisions: Evidence from Argentina," *Journal of Development Economics*, 97(2), 481–493.

Becker, G. (1971) *The Economics of Discrimination*, 1st ed. Chicago: University of Chicago Press.

Behar, A. and Freund, C. (2011). "The Trade Performance of the Middle East and North Africa," Middle East and North Africa Working Paper Series 53, Washington, DC: The World Bank.

Ben-Salem, M. and Zaki, C. (2019). "Revisiting the Impact of Trade Openness on Informal and Irregular Employment in Egypt," *Journal of Economic Integration*, 34(3), 465–497.

Bellakhal, R. and Mouelhi, R. (2023). "Digitalisation and Firm Performance: Evidence from Tunisian SMEs," *International Journal of Productivity and Quality Management*, 39(1), 42–65.

Bhagwati, J. N. (1995). "US Trade Policy: The Infatuation with FTAs," in C. Barfield (ed.), *The Dangerous Obsession with Free Trade Areas*, AEI.

Blyde, J. S. (2023). Your Assessment Is Welcome Here: The Trade Impacts of Mutual Recognition Agreements. *Applied Economics Letters*, 30(6), 796–802.

Bouët, A., Odjo, S. P. and Zaki, C. (2020) "African Agriculture Trade Monitor 2020," *International Food Policy Research Institute (IFPRI)*. https://www .ifpri.org/publication/africa-agriculture-trade-monitor-2020/.

Briguglio, L. (1995). "The Economy of a Small Island State Malta, 1960–1993," *Mediterranean World*, 14, 105–120.

Bruton, H. J. (1998). "A Reconsideration of Import Substitution," *Journal of Economic Literature*, 36(2), 903–936.

Chanda, R. (2017). "Trade in Services," in K. A. Reinert (ed.), *Handbook of Globalisation and Development*, Edward Elgar, 36–58.

Chaney, T. (2008). "Distorted Gravity: The Intensive and Extensive Margins of International Trade," *American Economic Review*, 98(4), 1707–1721.

Costinot, A. (2005). *Contract Enforcement, Division of Labor and the Pattern of Trade*. San Diego: Mimeo, University of California.

Costantini, V. and Liberati, P. (2014). "Technology Transfer, Institutions and Development," *Technological Forecasting and Social Change*, 88, 26–48.

Diop, N., Marotta, D. and de Melo, J. (2012). "Natural Resource Abundance, Growth, and Diversification in the Middle East and North Africa: The Effects of Natural Resources and the Role of Policies," World Bank Publications – Books, The World Bank Group, number 11956, December.

Dovis, M. and Zaki, C. (2020). "Global Value Chains and Business Environment: Which Factors Do Really Matter," *Review of Industrial Organization*, 57(2), 481–513.

Droguel, A. S. and Tekce, M. (2011). "Trade Liberalization and Export Diversification in Selected MENA Countries," *Topics in Middle Eastern and African Economies*, 13, 1–25.

Dollar, D. and Kraay, A. (2003). "Institutions, Trade, and Growth," *Journal of Monetary Economics*, 50(1), 133–162.

Dollar, D., Hallward-Driemeier, M. and Mengistae, T. (2004). "Investment Climate and International Integration", World Bank Policy Research Working Paper no. WPS3323, Washington, D.C., U.S.A.

El-Enbaby, H., Hendy, R. and Zaki, C. (2016). "Do SPS Measures Matter for Margins of Trade? Evidence from Firm-Level Data," *Applied Economics*, 48(21), 1949–1964.

Ezzat, A. and Zaki, C. (2022). "On the Political Economy of Trade Agreements: A *De Jure* and *De Facto* Analysis of the Effect of Institutions," *International Economics*, 172, 143–156.

Feenstra, R. C., Markusen, J. R. and Rose, A. K. (2001). "Using the Gravity Equation to Differentiate among Alternative Theories of Trade," *Canadian Journal of Economics*, 34, 430–447.

Feenstra, R. C. (2002). "Border Effects and the Gravity Equation: Consistent Methods for Estimation," *Scottish Journal of Political Economy*, 49(5, November), 491–506.

Fontagné, L., Orefice, G. and Piermartini, R. (2020). Making Small Firms Happy? The Heterogeneous Effect of Trade Facilitation Measures.*Review of International Economics*, 28(3), 565–598.

Frankel, J. A. and Romer, D. (2017). "Does Trade Cause Growth?" in *Global Trade*. Routledge, pp. 255–276.

Galal, A. (2008). *Industrial Policy in the Middle East and North Africa: Rethinking the Role of the State*. Cairo, Egypt: American University in Cairo Press.

Glick, R. and Taylor, A. M. (2008). "Collateral Damage: Trade Disruption and the Economic Impact of War," *NBER Working Paper 11565*, National Bureau of Economic Research, Cambridge.

Graham, F. D. (1923). "Some Aspects of Protection Further Considered," *Quarterly Journal of Economics*, 37(2), 199–227. https://doi.org/10.2307/1884763

Ghoneim, A. F. (2006). *Law Making for Trade Liberalization and Investment Promotion in Egypt. In The Imperative of Good Governance: Economic Reform, Political Will, Incentives, and Capacities for Meaningful*

Participation. Cairo: Economic Research Forum for the Arab Countries, Iran, and Turkey.

Goldberg, P. K., Khandelwal, A. K., Pavcnik, N. and Topalova, P. (2010). Imported Intermediate Inputs and Domestic Product Growth: Evidence from India. *The Quarterly Journal of Economics*, 125(4), 1727–1767.

Guedidi, I., Baghdadi, L. and Martínez-Zarzoso, I. (2025). "Trade Facilitation in Global Value Chains: Assessing the Role of Maritime Connectivity and Trading across Borders," *The Journal of International Trade & Economic Development*, 34(2), 309–339.

Guillin, A., Rabaud, I. and Zaki, C. (2023). "Does the Depth of Trade Agreements Matter for Trade in Services?" *The World Economy*, 46(12), 3616–3653.

Hendy, R. and Zaki, C. (2021). "Trade Facilitation and Firms' Exports: Evidence from Customs Data," *International Review of Economics and Finance*, 75, 197–209.

Hayo, B. and Caris, T. (2013). "Female Labour Force Participation in the MENA Region: The Role of Identity," *Review of Middle East Economics and Finance*, 9(3), 271–292.

Hvidt, M. (2013). "Import Substitution Industrialization and Economic Diversification: The Case of GCC Countries," Kuwait Programme on Development, Governance and Globalisation in the Gulf States, London School of Economics.

Heckscher, E. and Ohlin, B. (1933). *International and Inter-Regional Trade*. Cambridge, MA: Harvard University Press.

Heilmann, K. (2016). "Does Political Conflict Hurt Trade? Evidence from Consumer Boycotts," *Journal of International Economics*, 99, 179–191.

Helpman, E., Melitz, M. and Rubinstein, Y. (2008), "Estimating Trade Flows: Trading Partners and Trading Volumes," *Quarterly Journal of Economics*, 123(2), 441–487.

Jang, Y. J. (2018). How Do Mutual Recognition Agreements Influence Trade?. *Review of Development Economics*, 22(3), e95–e114.

Jaud, M. and Freund, C. (2015). *Champions Wanted: Promoting Exports in the Middle East and North Africa*. Washington, DC: World Bank Publications.

Jones, R. W. (1971). "A Three-Factor Model in Theory, Trade, and History," *The Journal of Political Economy*, 79(5), 903–908.

Juhász, R., Lane, N. J. and Rodrik, D. (2023). "The New Economics of Industrial Policy," *Annual Review of Economics*, 16, 213–242.

Kamal, Y. and Zaki, C. (2018). "How Do Technical Barriers to Trade Affect Egypt's Trade Margins," *Journal of Economic Integration*, 33(4), 659–721.

Karam, F. and Zaki, C. (2013). "On the Determinants of Trade in Services: Evidence from the MENA Region," *Applied Economics*, 45(33), 4626–4640.

Karam, F. and Zaki, C. (2015). "Trade Volume and Economic Growth in the MENA Region: Goods or Services?" *Economic Modelling*, 45, 22–37.

Karam, F. and Zaki, C. (2016). "How Did Wars Dampen Trade in the MENA Region?" *Applied Economics*, 48(60), 5909–5930.

Karam, F. and Zaki, C. (2019). "Why Don't MENA Countries Trade More? The Curse of Deficient Institutions," *The Quarterly Review of Economics and Finance*, 73, 56–77.

Karam, F. and Zaki, C. (2020). "A New Dawn for MENA Firms: Service Trade Liberalization for More Competitive Exports," *Applied Economics*, 52(1), 19–35.

Karam, F. and Zaki, C. (2021). "On Women Empowerment in International Trade: Impact on Firms' Productivity and Trade Margins in the MENA Region," *Journal of International Trade and Economic Development*, 30(3), 384–406.

Karam, F. and Zaki, C. (2021). "Trade and Economic Growth in the MENA Region: Do Trade in Goods and Trade in Services Differ in their Impact on Growth?" in H. Hakimian (ed.), *The Routledge Handbook on Middle Eastern Economy*. Routledge, pp. 165–186.

Karam, F. and Zaki, C. (2023). "When Trade Agreements are Gender-Friendly: Evidence from Firm-Level Data," LEO Working Paper Series, DR LEO 2023–19.

Karam, F. and Zaki, C. (2024). "When Trade Agreements Are Gender-Friendly: Impact on Women Empowerment using Firm Data", *Journal of Economic Integration*, 39(4), 875–898.

Kinda, T., Plane, P. and Veganzones-Varoudakis, M.A. (2009). "Firm's Productive Performance and the Investment Climate in Developing Economies: An Application to MENA Manufacturing," Policy research working paper no. 4869. The World Bank.

Krueger, A. O. (1990). "Asian Trade and Growth Lessons," *The American Economic Review*, 80(2), 108–112.

Krugman, P. (1979). "A Model of Innovation, Technology Transfer, and the World Distribution of Income," *Journal of Political Economy*, 87(2), 253–266. https://doi.org/10.1086/260748.

Krugman, P. (1980). "Scale Economies, Product Differentiation, and the Pattern of Trade," *The American Economic Review*, 70(5), 1944–7981.

Kruse, H. W., Martínez-Zarzoso, I. and Baghdadi, L. (2021). Standards and Political Connections: Evidence from Tunisia. *Journal of Development Economics*, 153, 102731.

Levchenko, A. A. (2007). "Institutional Quality and International Trade," *The Review of Economic Studies*, 74(3), 791–819.

López, R. A. (2005). "Trade and Growth: Reconciling the Macroeconomic and Microeconomic Evidence," *Journal of Economic Surveys*, 19(4), 623–648.

Luong, T. A. (2011). "The Impact of Input and Output Tariffs on Firms' Productivity: Theory and Evidence," *Review of International Economics*, 19(5), 821–835.

Martin, P., Mayer, T. and Thoenig, M. (2008). "Make Trade not War?" *Review of Economics Studies*, 75(3): 865–900.

Mattoo, A., Rocha, N. and Ruta, M. (2020). *The Handbook of Deep Trade Agreements*. Washington, DC: World Bank.

McCallum, J. (1995). "National Borders Matter: Canada-U.S. Regional Trade Patterns," *The American Economic Review*, 83(2), 615–662.

Melitz, M. J. (2003). "The Impact of Trade on Intra-Industry Reallocations and Aggregate Industry Productivity," *Econometrica, Econometric Society*, 71(6), 1695–1725.

Melitz, M. and Ottaviano, G. (2008). "Market Size, Trade and Productivity," *Review of Economic Studies*, 75, 295–316.

Marouani, M. A. and Mouelhi, R. (2016). "Contribution of Structural Change to Productivity Growth: Evidence from Tunisia," *Journal of African Economies*, 25(1), 110–132.

North, D. C. (1990). *Institutions, Institutional Change and Economic Performance*. Cambridge: Cambridge University Press.

OECD (2002). "Avantages pour les Entreprises de la Facilitation des Echanges," prepared by T. Matsudaira and Evokia Mosé, Working Party of the Trade Committee, TD/ TC/ WP(2001)21/ FINAL, August.

Prusa, T. J. (2001). "On the Spread and Impact of Anti-dumping," *Canadian Journal of Economics/Revue canadienne d'économique*, 34(3), 591–611.

Reinert, K. A. (2017). "Trade in Goods," in K. A. Reinert (ed.), *Handbook of Globalisation and Development*. Edward Elgar, pp. 19–35.

Ricardo, D. (1817). *On the Principles of Political Economy and Taxation*. Cambridge: Cambridge University Press.

Rodrik, D. (2005). "Growth Strategies," in P. Aghion and S. N. Durlauf (eds.), *Handbook of Economic Growth* (Vol. 1A, pp. 967–1014). Amsterdam: Elsevier.

Rouis, M. and Tabor, S. R. (2013). Regional Economic Integration in the Middle East and North Africa, Beyond Trade Reform. The World Bank. ISBN: 978–0–8213–9726–8.

Ruckteschler, C., Malik, A. and Eibl, F. (2022). Politics of Trade Protection in an Autocracy: Evidence from an EU Tariff Liberalization in Morocco. *European Journal of Political Economy*, 71, 102063.

Samuelson, P. A. (1971). "Ohlin Was Right." *The Swedish Journal of Economics*, 73(4), 365–384.

Sinani, E. and Meyer, K. E. (2004). "Spillovers of Technology Transfer from FDI: The Case of Estonia," *Journal of Comparative Economics*, 32(3), 445–466.

Smith, A. (1776). "An Inquiry into the Nature and Causes of the Wealth of Nations," History of Economic Thought Books, McMaster University Archive for the History of Economic Thought, number smith1776.

Selwaness, I. and Zaki, C. (2015). "Assessing the Impact of Trade Reforms on informal employment in Egypt, *The Journal of North African Studies*, vol. 20(3), pages 391–414.

Stolper, W. and Samuelson, P. A. (1941). "Protection and Real Wages," *Review of Economic Studies*, 9, 58–73.

Selwaness, I. and Zaki, C. (2019). "On the Interaction between Exports and Labor Market Regulations: Evidence from the MENA Countries," *Quarterly Review of Economics and Finance*, 73, 24–33.

Tinbergen, J. (1962). *Shaping the World Economy: Suggestions for an International Economic Policy.* New York: The Twentieth Century Fund.

Viner, J. (1953). "Cost Curves and Supply Curves," In G. J. Stigler and K. E. Boulding (eds.), *Readings in Price Theory.* London: Allen and Unwin, pp. 198–232.

World Bank (2024). *World Development Report 2024: The Middle-Income Trap.* Washington, DC: World Bank. https://doi.org/10.1596/978-1-4648-2078-6. License: Creative Commons Attribution CC BY3.0 IGO.

WDI (2024). World Development Indicators database, the World Bank. https://databank.worldbank.org/source/world-development-indicators#.

Zaki, C. (2014). "On Trade Policies and Wage Disparity in Egypt: Evidence from Microeconomic Data," *International Economic Journal*, 28(1), 37–69.

Zaki, C. (2017) "Making International Trade Easier: A Survey of the Trade Facilitation Effects," *Review of Economics and Political Science*, 2(2), 25–55.

Zaki, C. (2021). "Why Egypt's Trade Policy Failed to Improve Its External's Competitiveness?" in R. Springborg, A. I. Saad, A. I. Ahmed Adly, A. P. Gorman, T. Moustafa, N. Sakr and S. Smierciak (eds.), *Routledge Handbook of Contemporary Egypt.*

Zaki, C. (2023). "Does Digitalization Matter? Evidence from Egyptian and Jordanian Firms," ERF Working Paper No. 1636.

Cambridge Elements

International Economics

Kenneth A. Reinert

George Mason University

Kenneth A. Reinert is Professor of Public Policy in the Schar School of Policy and Government at George Mason University where he directs the Global Commerce and Policy master's degree program. He is author of *An Introduction to International Economics: New Perspectives on the World Economy* with Cambridge University Press and coauthor of *Globalization for Development: Meeting New Challenges* with Oxford University Press. He is also editor of *The Handbook of Globalisation and Development* with Edward Elgar and co-editor of the two-volume *Princeton Encyclopedia of the World Economy* with Princeton University Press.

About the Series

International economics is a distinct field with both fundamental theoretical insights and increasing empirical and policy relevance. The *Cambridge Elements in International Economics* showcases this field, covering the subfields of international trade, international money and finance, and international production, and featuring both established researchers and new contributors from all parts of the world. It aims for a level of theoretical discourse slightly above that of the *Journal of Economic Perspectives* to maintain accessibility. It extends Cambridge University Press' established reputation in international economics into the new, digital format of *Cambridge Elements*. It attempts to fill the niche once occupied by the *Princeton Essays in International Finance*, a series that no longer exists.

There is a great deal of important work that takes place in international economics that is set out in highly theoretical and mathematical terms. This new Elements does not eschew this work but seeks a broader audience that includes academic economists and researchers, including those working in international organizations, such as the World Bank, the International Monetary Fund, and the Organization for Economic Cooperation and Development.

For EU product safety concerns, contact us at Calle de José Abascal, 56–1°,
28003 Madrid, Spain or eugpsr@cambridge.org.